SPORTS PSYCHOLOGY

FOR ATHLETES

Think Like a Champion
and Train Like a Warrior

5-IN-1 BUNDLE

This book includes:

Mental Toughness
Intermittent Fasting
Bodybuilding
Strength Training
Body Weight Training

"First Train the Mind, Then Train the Body"
— *Epic Rios*

Mental Toughness

How to be a Badass in Sports, Business, and Life

Table of Contents

There are no scenarios in which the publisher or the original author of this work can be in any fashion deemed liable for any hardship or damages that may befall them after undertaking information described herein.

Additionally, the information in the following pages is intended only for informational purposes and should thus be thought of as universal.

As befitting its nature, it is presented without assurance regarding its prolonged validity or interim quality.

Trademarks that are mentioned are done without written consent and can in no way be considered an endorsement from the trademark holder.

Introduction

Congratulations on downloading *Mental Toughness* and thank you for doing so.

The following chapters will discuss what mental toughness is and how it is going to change your life. You will learn what mental toughness is and how to build it. Not only that but how it will be effective in business and sports.

There are plenty of books on this subject on the market that you could have chosen, thanks again for choosing this one! Every effort was made to ensure it is full of as much useful information as possible; and please enjoy!

Chapter one: What is Mental Toughness

What is mental toughness? Mental toughness is defined as the measure of the resilience and confidence that one has that is going to be part of predicting that person's success in sports, education, and in the workplace.

Mental toughness first came around with the training that is done for sports due to the attributes that enable someone to become a better athlete so that they can deal with the difficult training and competitive situations that are going to come about from playing sports without that person losing their confidence.

As time has gone on, the term has begun to be used not only by those who work with athletes but by business leaders as well.

Quite often, the term mental toughness is used to describe a set of positive attributes that are going to assist someone in coping with situations that are difficult to deal with. Coaches and many sports commentators use it as a way to talk about an athlete's mental state as they overcome a difficult circumstance in order to succeed.

But, over the past fifteen years, researchers have tried to come up with a scientific definition for mental toughness so that criteria could be established as a way to measure mental toughness in order for analysis and comparisons to be made. Three different teams have been able to come up with a definition for mental toughness.

Jones, Hanton, and Connaughton

"Mental toughness is having the natural or developed psychological edge that enables you to generally cope better than your opponents with the many demands (competition, training, lifestyle) that a sport places on a performer, specifically to be more consistent and better than your opponents in remaining determined, focused, confident, and in control under pressure."

Clough and Earle

This team of researchers decided that mental toughness was a personality trait that consisted of several components. These components were: commitment, confidence, control, challenge. If you had each of these personality traits then you had the mental toughness trait.

Gucciardi, Gordon, and Dimmock

"Mental toughness in Australian Football is a collection of values, attitudes, behaviors, and emotions that enable you to persevere and overcome any obstacle, adversity, or pressure experienced, but also to maintain concentration and motivation when things are going well to consistently achieve your goals."

There are a few psychologists that are arguing that there are different definitions when it comes to mental toughness and how it is developed.

Some attributes of those who are mentally tough are going to be different from those that are not developing their mental toughness.

One of the differences is that if you are a male or female, your mental toughness is going to be different from your significant other due to your gender.

It is also going to depend on if you are someone who has to work with others every day or if you work by yourself and barely have contact with others.

In studies that have been done specifically for sports and the mental toughness of athletes, it shows that there is not a common framework between sports such as cricket and soccer, but the definition for mental toughness that was given in the Jones study as well as the Gucciardi study are close to the actual definition of what mental toughness is.

A lot of the studies that focus on sports are going to be using the model that was provided by Clough so that there are samples from the athletes that are studied so that links can be shown between the mental toughness of the athlete along with how they cope with the stress they are under, their psychological skills, how they perform, and their emotional reactivity.

A study that was published shows that athletes are going to follow the four C's model. It also shows that the junior colleagues in businesses are not going to be as tough as the senior managers.

Researchers are currently in an active debate about if mental toughness is a characteristic that is developed or if it is something that comes from your genetics.

Two studies that have been done show that there is a foundational process that occurs when a person begins developing their mental toughness throughout their life.

For example, when a study was done on soccer players, their parents, and their coaches, the parents are going to give a generalized form of mental toughness that the coaches are going to continue to build on so that the athlete is mentally tough for their sport.

In a similar study, the mental toughness of a person is going to be developed first through their development of a tough attitude, and for athletes this is going to come through focus and a strong belief in themselves while they are practicing and training for their games and competitions.

It is easier to understand if you equate mental toughness to things such as hardiness or resilience.

The term resilience is often times used incorrectly to describe mental toughness, but there are psychologists that have defined resilience as the ability to positively adapt to a stressful situation.

Hardiness is a similar construct to mental toughness, though, and it is usually a personality trait that is constructed and seen throughout someone's life.

This is going to be different from the concept of mental toughness that was provided by Jones and Gucciardi.

It was these authors who thought that mental toughness made someone unstable and the development of mental toughness was going to fluctuate overtime therefore varying from each person and the situation that they were placed in.

This definition plagues the use of the term for mental toughness and should mental toughness only exist as a valid construct then it is going to depend on maladaptive.

However, evidence has been found that supports the concept of mental toughness being derived from behaviors that are over trained.

In 2009, two instruments were developed and validated to measure mental toughness.

The colleagues of Gucciardi and himself validated the AFMTI (American Football Mental Toughness Inventory) while at the same time the SMTQ (Sports Mental Toughness Questionnaire) was validated by Sheard and Golby.

MTQ48 came before the AFMTI and SMTQ by seven years.

The structure of MTQ48 is supported by research groups that are independently run by Horsburgh.

It was Dr. Lee Crust from the University of Lincoln that comparted SMTQ to MTQ48 and discovered that both of them tapped into the core components of mental toughness, however MTQ48 provided a better measure of one's mental toughness.

Chapter two: How to Develop Mental Toughness

Even if you do not believe that you have mental toughness, you are going to be able to build mental toughness.

In having mental toughness, you are going to be empowered and you will then be able to bounce back from the bad quicker and you are going to be stronger than you were before.

1. Move straight to acceptance: whenever you are wanting a specific outcome from a situation, you are going to need to accept when you do not get the outcome that you wanted.

    When you allow the different outcome to overtake you, you set yourself back and you create a resistance that is going to slow you down in the long run.

    Therefore, even if you do not like what has happened, you are going to have to accept that it happened and move on.

2. Reframe the situation: it is human nature to be upset whenever things do not go the way that you want them to.

    But, with mental toughness you are going to be able to persevere even though things are going the exact opposite of how you are wanting them to go.

One way to overcome allowing situations to bring you down is to look at the obstacle that you are facing and think of how you are going to be able to prove yourself in overcoming that obstacle.

3. Shifting to solution mode: rather than allowing the difficult situation that you did not plan for to overtake you and make it to where you are unable to think of anything other than the fact that you did not get the outcome that you wanted, then you are going to be harming yourself.

   Therefore, when you get an outcome that you did not want or expect, you should instantly override the tendency to focus on what is going wrong and shift your focus to trying to find a solution to solve your problem.

Keep in mind that mental toughness is about overcoming difficult situations that you are placed in whether by accident or because it is what life throws at you.

It is human nature to panic and focus on everything bad that is happening. However, with mental toughness, you are going to be able to push past that panic and begin to look for a solution to fix the issue.

Chapter three: Mental Toughness – Why it is Important and Why it is Useful

Mental toughness is important because it can help assist someone who is going through a tough situation get through it easier because they are not going to allow the bad to overcome them.

With mental toughness, they are going to be able to succeed in one way or another.

Even if you do not succeed in the way that you expect yourself to, you are going to be able to find solutions that others may not see due to the fact that they are focused on the bad that is occurring.

With mental toughness, you are going to be healthier mentally because you are not allowing the bad situations to overtake your thoughts.

When you allow the bad to control your life, you end up becoming depressed which affects the rest of your life.

So, in essence, you are going to be improving your attitude and performing to the best of your abilities in anything that you try to do.

Here is how mental toughness is going to be useful to you in your life.

1. Improves focus and one's ability to deal with distractions: you will be able to concentrate without your focus being displaced to the wrong area.

2. Grow confidence: when you do not have confidence, you are going to be doubting yourself and when you doubt yourself you are not going to perform as you should.

   Doubt typically indicates that someone has low self-confidence or is sabotaging his own confidence before they even start their task. But having confidence is going to be vital because it is not only going to determine other mental skills you are going to need to have, but your performance as well.

3. Skills to cope with errors and setbacks: having control of your emotions is going to be the number one thing that you need to do in order to get yourself in the zone to complete what you need to complete.

   Any expectations that you have need to be addressed so that you can stay composed as you find yourself under pressure despite the fact that you are probably going to end up making mistakes or have things that are going to set you back and frustrate you.

4. The right zone of intensity: you do not need to be intense in some situations but in other situations you do need to be intense.

It is important that you find the right intensity so that you are able to find that line that sits between being over excited and excited.

5. Communication and cohesion: having mental toughness is going to make it to where you can work well with other people and communicate ideas and thoughts with them.

    The better that you are able to communicate and work with others, the easier your life is going to be and the better the results that you receive will be.

6. Instill a healthy belief system and identify irrational thoughts: there are always going to be beliefs that people have that are going to be ineffective and the attitudes that are not only going to place self-labels on one that are negative, but also how to get people out of their comfort zones that keep them from performing to the best of their ability.

    You will be replacing your unhealthy beliefs with a new way of thinking. You are going to be stuck if you do not get rid of the unhealthy or irrational beliefs no matter how hard you try.

7. Improve motivation: when you look at your level of motivation, you need to think of why you are doing what you are doing.

    There are going to be some motivators that will be better for your long-term goals than others will be.

    If you are motivated for the wrong reasons then you are not going to be performing the best that you can. Instead, you need to find your motivation that motivates you for the right reasons.

8. Confidence after a setback: with mental toughness, you are going to have the confidence that you need to get back up after you have a setback.

    If you do not have strong mental toughness, you are going to allow your setbacks to stop you from trying again.

In the end, mental toughness is going to make it to where you can keep going when things do not go your way. Not only that, but you are going to be improving your mental faculties.

Anyone is going to be able to develop mental toughness and use it in every aspect of their life. It does not matter who you are, all it takes is a little bit of motivation in order to develop mental toughness.

Mental toughness can be used in sports, education, and business despite the fact that it is commonly talked about that with sports.

If you are in sports, you can take the mental toughness that your coach teaches you and apply it to other parts of your life.

Chapter four: How to Use Mental Toughness

Mental toughness can be used in every area of your life.

It does not matter if you are using it in sports or in business, mental toughness is something you are going to want to have so that you can improve every aspect of your life.

Sports

In sports, athletes are going to be put under an intense amount of pressure in which they are likely to become stressed out because they want to do well and win the game. This stressful mentality may begin when someone starts sports at a young age.

Using mental toughness in sports is going to make it to where the athlete is able to figure out just how intense they need to go at the game that they are playing.

Mental toughness is going to make it to where the athlete is going to be able to face his opponent even if they are bigger than him.

And, rather than to be scared of the person that they are facing, they are going to be able to go up against them and do their best.

Sports require a high level of focus so that the athlete is able to perform their best, and if they do not have mental toughness, then they are not going to be performing their best.

Coaches are going to work on building their teams' mental toughness not only so that they can help their team in other areas of their life, but also so that their team works together better and they are able to communicate in an effort to win their game.

Business

All businesses depend on the clients that work with them in order to make sure that the business continues to make a profit.

It is easy to allow the loss of a client or a contract not coming up the way that you are wanting it to be to overtake your emotions and cause you to be emotional and then that emotional level is going to overtake your other deals and cause you to possibly tank those as well.

So, whenever a client backs out of a deal that you have set up with them, instead of allowing it to break you, you will start to look at the other side of things and find a solution for what has happened.

Mental toughness is going to make it to where you can focus on the problem that you are facing, but you do not allow it to break you.

To bust through stereotypes

Every person in the world stereotypes.

It is human nature to look at someone and automatically put a label on them even if it is not right as to who they truly are.

Breaking these stereotypes is tough, however, you are going to be able to use your newfound mental toughness in order to break though the negative thoughts, bias, and stereotypes that come so easily to everyone.

1. Realize that your brain has a confirmation bias built in: what this means is that your brain is going to automatically store information that matches your beliefs, self-image, and values.

   This memory system makes it to where your brain gets overloaded from too much information.

   There is research that shows that people like to believe that their beliefs are logical, rational, and objective.

   However, in reality, your beliefs are typically based on any sort of information you have gotten that confirms your ideas while ignoring any information you might receive that challenges those beliefs.

General beliefs are going to be unstable due to the fact that any information that comes to light is going to cause you to change your belief as you educate yourself.

While your generalizations are going to change over time, they are going to also influence how you respond to the situations that happen around you in order to identify the generalizations that are going to assist you in reacting with accuracy and resilience.

2. How stereotypes affect performance: stereotype threats are going to happen whenever negative stereotypes weaken your confidence therefore causing you to meet an

obstacle that is going to stand in your way of achieving success.

For example, most times women in school are steered away from science and math fields because they are supposed to be more for men.

Therefore, women move to other fields where it is more sociably accepted for them to work.

On the other hand, stereotypes can be good as well.

In one case that researchers have discovered is that women of Asian American decent will do better on math tests than women who are not Asian.

This stereotype made it to where the Asian American women have their confidence boosted which helps them to do better on the math tests.

3. Know your burdens and your barriers: when you are faced with a negative stereotype, you will be developing your mental toughness in order for you to be able to acknowledge where your barriers are and what your burdens are.

One study done in 2012 showed that when you stretch your mind in an effort to come up with solutions that are not as predictable or mundane your creativity is going to be stimulated while improving your mental flexibility.

As you strengthen your mentality, you will be able to figure out what your burdens are and where your barriers are without needing to give up the hopes you have for future success.

Whenever you acknowledge your burdens and barriers, you will be:

1. Cultivating a mindset that is flexible and is going to counteract any stereotype threats that come your way.

2. You will create strategies that are going to be effective in dealing with negative stereotypes.

3. You will be stimulating your creativity.

4. Cognitive performance will improve.

5. Thinking that is flexible will be encouraged.

6. You will change how you see yourself.

Everyday life

As you have seen in the previous sections, you are going to be able to use mental toughness to face any situation that is difficult.

You will be changing the way that you think from negative to positive therefore changing how you react to situations that you come up against.

Chapter five: Mental Toughness and Your Health, Your Work, and Your Life

What is the difference between someone who is able to accomplish their goals and someone who does not accomplish their goals?

Typically, the answer is because they have something that the other person does not have.

They are faster or they have a better work ethic than someone else. However, it has more to do than just your intelligence level and your talent.

There is research that shows that your mental toughness is going to play the biggest role when it comes to achieving any goals that you have in life, in your job, and in your health.

This is good news due to the fact that it allows you to know that it is not going to be something that you are born with, rather it is going to be something you are able to develop and work on.

When you are looking at your health, you can be healthy or you can be trying to get healthy, but your mental toughness is going to be part of what makes it to where you are going to be able to strive to reach those goals after you have set them.

For example, if you are wanting to be able to run a 5k, then you are going to begin training for it, and in order to keep up with your training as well as be able to finally make that 5k run, you are going to use your mental toughness to tell yourself that you are going to keep going when you feel like you want to give in.

In the end, you are going to feel better about yourself because you are going to have stuck to your guns and achieved the goal that you were wanting to achieve.

This is going to be the same for your work and your life. Anything that you want to get done is going to take mental toughness to accomplish.

Want to get that big client for your job so that you are able to get the bonus that your boss has promised as well as bring in more business for your company?

You are going to use your mental toughness in order to get the client. Even if they do not like what you have to offer them, you will have the mentality that is going to make it to where you automatically come up with a solution that is going to be beneficial to you both.

This is going to be the same for any other aspect of your life.

For example, if you are wanting to graduate with honors from school, you are going to need to use your mental toughness in order to ensure that you get good grades in school and that you are doing everything that you need in order to meet the criteria that is going to be set up by your school so that you are able to graduate with honors.

Just because you have mental toughness does not mean that things are going to come easily for you, it just means that you are going to have the mental endurance that it is going to take in order to get the job done.

You are not going to be allowing the negative to keep you from achieving what it is that you are wanting to achieve because you are going to be able to think of solutions and look at the positive side of things rather than seeing a difficult situation and backing away, instead you are going to face it head on and overcome it!

Chapter six: Mental Toughness and How the Military, Athletes, and Businessmen Use It

Each and every year there are over a thousand different cadets that are entering West Point, the United States Military Academy with the dream of joining the military.

The first summer that these cadets spend on campus means that they have to pass a series of tests that are going to test them to ensure that they are the right material that the military is looking for.

The initiation that occurs over the summer is known as Beast Barracks.

Some researchers went to West Point and studied the Best Barracks to see how the test worked.

It was discovered that the test was engineered specifically to test just how far they are going to be able to push a cadet not only physically, but mentally and emotionally as well.

Those that are able to complete the testing are the cadets who are more intelligent, are bigger, and are stronger than those that do not complete the testing.

A researcher at the University of Pennsylvania discovered that those that succeeded versus those that did not whenever she started tracking the cadets of West Point.

The cadets that were able to pass the test showed exactly how mental toughness and passion as well as perseverance impact one's ability to achieve their goals.

In the class that was observed there were over two thousand cadets that came into West Point in two different classes.

The researcher took their rank in their graduating class from high school, their Leadership Potential Score as well as their SAT score along with their Physical Aptitude Exam and placed it on the grit scale to see how likely it was that they were going to be able to complete the Best Barracks.

The results were that those who completed the testing were not necessarily the strongest or smartest, they did it even have the best leadership potential, instead it was the cadets who had the most grit that found themselves finishing the Beast Barracks.

Those cadets that were scoring higher on the grit scale were the ones that had a higher percentage of finishing their testing over those who did not score high on the grit test.

In essence, it was the cadets who showed that they had mental toughness over those who were stronger and more intelligent that ended up succeeding at West Point.

Athletes

An athlete is going to use mental toughness to overcome the brutal circumstances that they face when they are training and playing the game.

Many professional athletes have a very rigorous training schedule that usually means that they are harming themselves even though it is not intentional.

Many times, it is going to be easy for an athlete to say that they are done and give up, however, they do not do that.

Mental toughness or grit is going to be what separates those that do not make it into the pros because they do not have what it takes to deal with the pressure that comes with being a professional athlete.

As a professional athlete, you not only have to deal with the pressure that comes from the coaches for you to do better each time that you practice, but the pressure from the fans and your team mates.

Your mental toughness is going to help you cope with that pressure so that you do not buckle under it and you do not break down in the middle of a game in front of thousands of fans.

Instead, your grit is going to tell you that you are going to do your best even if you lose, you are going to perform the best that you can so that you can look back at that game and say that you did your absolute best.

Your grit is also going to tell you that if you did not perform your absolute best, that you will next time.

Therefore, the next practice that you have with your team, your communication is going to be better and you are going to do everything that you can to do better than you did in the game.

Business men

Just for a second imagine that you are sitting in your office at a big company and your boss walks in telling you that if you land this particular client that he is going to make you a partner and you will never have to want for money again.
You will be set for the rest of your life, even after you retire.

What are you going to do?

Well, you are not going to go straight to that client without having a plan to entice them into signing a contract with your company, that is for sure!

Instead, you are going to come up with a plan that is going to be virtually foolproof in your opinion so that you are able to get that client to sign with you so that you can become partner.

You are going to come up with solutions to anything that you can imagine would go wrong and cause the client to not sign with your company.

You may not know it, but you are using your mental toughness to prepare yourself for your big meeting with this client and thinking on the positive side of things and believing that you are going to be making the best choice not only for you but for your company too.

Your mental toughness is going to be what helps you in the meeting because you are going to be using the power of your mind to overcome the odds and do what others believe is impossible.

In the end, it does not matter how charming you are, how smart you are, or how strong you are, your grit is going to be what determines how successful you are.

Your grit is going to be what pushes you to perform your absolute best in any situation that you are placed in.

Chapter seven: What Makes Someone Mentally Tough?

As you have seen in previous chapters, mental toughness is something that you are going to be able to develop.

But, what happens when our mental toughness is challenged? How do we know we are tough enough mentally to make the decision that will lead us to success?

Whenever you feel stuck, it is hard to remain mentally tough so that you can continue to break the mold and stand out in the crowd.

Just because you are mentally tough does not mean that you are exempt from mistakes. Remember what Thomas Edison said in 1914: "Thank goodness all our mistakes were burned up. Now we can start fresh again."

We should all strive to have the mental toughness of Edison, and here is what will symbolize that you are a mentally tough person.

1. You have emotional intelligence.

   When it comes down to it, being emotionally intelligent is the cornerstone of have mental toughness.

This means that you understand and have full control over your negative emotions and are able to do something productive with those emotions.

Whenever your mental toughness is tested, so is your emotional intelligence.

While your IQ is a fixed number, your emotional IQ is a skill that is flexible and you can improve with a little bit of effort.

2. Confidence is a must.

    Henry Ford said, "Whether you think you can, or think you can't, you're right."

    It is your mentality that is going to determine if you are going to be able to succeed or not and it is not just something that is said to give people more motivation, it is a fact.

    In a study that was done at the Melbourne University, confident people tended to move on in life and earn higher wages while also getting promoted quicker than others did.

    Having true confidence is going to look different than those who have false confidence and use it to hide their insecurities.

    People who are mentally tough are going to have the upper hand over those are doubt their own confidence.

3. Toxic people are neutralized.

   No one likes dealing with people who are frustrating.

   But, those who are mentally tough can control the interactions that they have with those around them.

   Whenever a mentally tough person comes in contact with someone who is toxic, they are able to control their emotions and do not allow the negative emotions that will arise to add to the chaos.

   They also look at the other person's point of view and find common ground to try and come up with a solution to any problem.

4. They embrace change.

   People who are mentally tough are going to be flexible and adapt when things change even though change can be scary and could be a threat to their happiness.

   Change is constantly around the corner so they make a plan that is going to be put into place whenever change does happen.

5. They aren't afraid to say no.

   Research done in San Francisco at the University of California showed that the less you say no, the more stress you are going experience.

   But, someone who is mentally tough will say no and be healthy and have a high self-esteem, their no's are going to be clear and they will avoid phrases such as "I am not certain" or "I do not think I can."

6. Fear is the number one source of people's regrets.

   Those who are mentally tough are going to know that they are going to regret the chances that they never took.

   Therefore, they are going to be ones who take more risks so that they do not have regrets later in life.

Chapter eight: Examples of Mental Toughness

While we have talked about mental toughness and how it is used, what are some examples of mental toughness?

Who do we know or have we heard about that has shown us an example of mental toughness?

Mental toughness is not something that needs to be shown by example, but it does make it easier to stick to developing your own mental toughness when you know that someone you look up to has shown you a good example and is going to be someone that you strive to emulate.

1. In the World Series of 1956, pitcher Don Larson pitched a perfect game in game five.

    This was the only perfect game ever recorded in history!

    But, it was during game two of the same series where he only picked 1.2 innings and ended up costing his team the game 13 to 8.

    This shows that Don Larson had mental toughness because he took a setback (the loss in game two) and allowed it to motivate him to pitch a perfect game later therefore showing that he was able to overcome the loss and work better with his team.

2. Raymond Berry retired from the NFL as an all-time reception leader having only caught thirteen passes in his rookie year playing for the Colts.

   Berry showed mental toughness by becoming the only person who caught that many passes in his rookie year.

   He did not allow the pressure of being in the NFL stop him from proving that he was the best of the best.

3. One of the greatest tennis players of all time, Roger Federer, won not just one but seven Wimbledon titles.

   However, he lost the very first round of Wimbledon in the first three years that he played.

   Roger Federer's mental toughness came from being pushed forward to do better each time that he made it to Wimbledon.

   Even though he lost his first three years, he did not let that stop him, instead, he kept playing and went on to prove that he deserved those titles that he won.

4. At the age of fifteen, Taylor Swift was denied a contract by RCA. Now, she is one of the biggest pop/country singers that there is. She did not let one denial stop her from singing and achieving her dreams.

5. The first three Grand Slam Finals that Andre Agassi played, he lost. But, due to his mental toughness, he did not stop playing and continued to play and went on to win!

6. Minnesota Vikings Jim Marshall recovered a fumble and ran the wrong way.

   When he realized what he was doing, he threw the ball out of bounds for a safety and so that the other team would not get a touchdown.

   The next play, Marshall forced a fumble by sacking the quarterback.

   A team mate of Marshall picked up the fumble and got the touchdown that helped the Vikings win the game.

   Despite the fact that Marshall fouled up, he was able to fix his mistake and lead his team for a win.

7. In 1988 Mat Biondi lost his first two finals in the Olympic Games. However, he ended up winning five gold medals later in the games proving that his mental toughness was high enough that his losses did not set him back therefore making it to where he was able to earn his gold medals.

8. Trace Adkins was shot by his ex-wife.

   The bullet went through both of his lungs and his heart and yet he survived because he was mentally tough.

   Now, Trace Adkins is one of the biggest country singers that there is.

9. Danielle Ballengee showed she was mentally tough whenever she went on to finish fifth in a sixty mile race that involved mountain biking, orienteering, rope courses,

running, and kayaking after falling from a sixty foot cliff and being stranded for two days.

She suffered from a shattered pelvis and internal bleeding. The race was a hundred and fifty days after her accident and ninety of those days she spent in a wheel chair.

10. At the age of nineteen Lady Gaga was signed with a record company, however, they let her go three months into her contract.

Even though she had to deal with the setback, she ended up becoming one of the biggest singers known worldwide.

11. If George Washington had not been mentally tough he would not have become our first president due to the fact that he suffered a huge set back!

Washington actually lost his first battle. If he had not been mentally tough then he would have allowed this loss to define him and we would be living in a much different country.

While that is just a few of what some of the people that we look up to have done to prove their mental toughness, how can you use your mental toughness?

Some of the things that you can do to show your mental toughness are:

1. Do a twenty-four hour fast even if you do not need to.

You are going to be showing discipline and will be able to do it when you need to for your health.

2. Exercise each day for a month.

   Not only is the month that you exercise going to create a routine, but you are going to make it to where your body is going to crave the exercise that you have been putting yourself through.

   Therefore, if you are to stop, your body is going to demand that you start it back up.

3. Meditate every morning.

   Creating this ritual is going to not only work on your discipline, but it is also going to make it to where you are going to have time to visualize what it is that you are wanting to do as well as helping you remain calm.

These are just a few examples of things that you can do to show your mental toughness, but there are plenty of other examples that you are going to be able to figure out so that you find one that is going to meet your needs.

You are not going to have to do something physical every day.

You could also do something like the crossword every Sunday or practicing a musical instrument.

Chapter nine: Strategies for Strengthening and Improving Mental Toughness

If you have already developed your mental toughness, then you are going to want to make sure that you have a strong mental state as well as be able to improve it so that you are not going to fall victim to not having mental toughness which can lead to you having a hard time getting it back.

To build your mental toughness, you are going to see a few exercises that you can do that will also make it to where you strengthen your mental toughness.

1. Increase your confidence.

Challenge yourself with a skill that you have not fully mastered every day.

The more confidence that you have in your skills, the better that you are going to be able to use that skill.

Not only that, but you are going to gain the confidence to do almost anything without worrying about if you are going to be able to or not.

2. Embrace your sense of duty

You do not have to be in the military to have a sense of duty.

No matter what job you do, you are going to have a sense of duty.

Take a piece of paper and write down the description for your job and any other role that you may have in your life.

Review the descriptions each week and find things that you can do to fulfill that job description.

For example, as a mother, you are going to have to make sure that your family is fed.

So, instead of going to the store and buying frozen meals, cook something for them!

3. Do for your team

Write down the names of everyone you trust no matter who they are to you.

Under each name write down at least two things that you can do to strenghten your bond with that person.

4. Find pride

Find things that you are proud of in your life.

It does not have to be something major, as long as you are proud of it, that is all that matters.

Whenever you feel like you are slipping in your mental toughness, look at that list and rediscover why you are proud of yourself and what you should be proud of so that you can continue to move forward and find success.

Once you have gotten your mental toughness developed, you are going to want to increase your mental toughnes so that it is never not being used.

Increasing your mental toughness is going to be like exercising each day, it is something that needs to be done in order to make sure that you are not allowing it to just sit there and not be used.

1. Focus on the present

Sometimes it is hard to focus on what is going on in the present because of everything that is going on around us.

However, when you force yourself to focus on taking the next step, one at a time, rather than planning out everything, you are going to be focusing on what is happening now rather than what is going to happen or what has happened.

2. Have a short memory

Do not dwell on the mistakes that you have made in the past.

Learn from the mistakes that you make and keep moving on.

If you dwell on what has happened, then you are going to be living in the past and therefore you are not going to be able to achieve your goal due to the fact that you are not allowing yourself to keep your eye on the prize.

3. Remain positive

Do not let the negative overtake you.

The world is full of negative but having control of your emotions is going to make it to where you are able to let go of that negative and replace it with positive.

Staying positive is going to assist you as you try to achieve your goals. Rather than wondering if you will reach your goal, you will be telling yourself that you can do it!

4. Become a ritual-aholic

Stick to the good rituals. Find the rituals that are going to help condition you for what it is that you are wanting to do.

5. Visualize your future

You are going to change whether you like it or not.

Having strong mental toughness is going to be the key in changing your future.

Think and picture your future the way tha you are wanting it to be and work towards it.

Visualizing is going to be a big key to reaching for the stars. As Christian Nevell said: "It is the nature of thought to find its way into action."

6. Change the crowd you associate with

If you are wanting to be the CEO of a company, you are not going to want to associate yourself with those who do not have jobs or are doing things that are going to end up getting you in trouble just by associating with them.

Therefore, you are going to want to associate yourself with people who are going to help you to achieve your goals.

As an athlete it is often said if you want to be a winner, you are going to want to hang around winners. The same is true in every aspect of your life.

7. Repeat your affirmations

Repeating your affirmations is a good way to remind yourself of what it is that you are trying to do.

You are going to be changing the way that you think so that you can remind yourself that you are doing the right thing as you keep yourself on track and remove all of those negative thoughts with the positive ones.

8. Read a good book

This is a ritual that is going to make it to where you can expand your mind and give you new ideas.

Besides, it is going to be a better way to fall asleep over watching violence that many people see when they fall asleep watching the news.

9. Keep yourself calm

It is easy to allow yourself to overreact and let your emotions get the best of you.

However, it is going to be better for you in the long run to keep yourself calm in situations where you would normally overreact because you are going to be showing that you have control over your emotions.

Keeping yourself calm is also going to be conditioning yourself so that you do not have to worry about allowing the negative emotions and thoughts to pop up and destroy all of the hard work that you have done.

Some other things that you can do is to ensure that you are being flexible as well as being resilient.

Physical exercise can also be used as a way to increase your mental toughness.

Chapter ten: Qualities of a Mentally Tough Person

People who are mentally tough are going to have a specific set of qualities that are going to set them apart from other people.

These qualities are going to be part of what makes it to where these people are mentally tough because they are going to be developing these skills as they go about developing their mental toughness.

1. People who are mentally tough are going to be competitive.

   They look at things as a competition because they want to prove not only to themselves but also to others that they are better than what they used to be and that they are going to be able to move forward with what they are wanting to achieve.

   They are not competitive just to prove that they can win, they are proving that they are not going to let something set them back and keep them from getting what they want.

   Even if they lose, they are not going to let it set them back in what they are trying to do.

2. They have the ability to bounce back.

   As just discussed, someone who is mentally tough is going to make it to where what sets them back isn't going to keep them there.

   Instead, someone who is mentally tough is going to use that set back and motivate them to push foward and keep going even if they feel like giving up.

3. Composure is important due to the fact that mentally tough people often find themselves in situations that are going to be high pressure.

   If they do not keep their composure, they are likely to crack under that pressure. Therefore the composure is going to make it to where they are able to deal with the pressure no matter how much is placed on them.

4. Focus is important as well because it is going to help someone who is mentally tough to keep their eyes on the prize, that way they are able to keep going and keep finding solutions to be able to achieve their goal.

   That focus is going to come into play later on due to the fact that the better they are able to focus the easier it is going to be for them to be able to use that focus on other things that are going on in their life.

5. A mentally tough person has high impact in leadership because they prove that they are able to step up and deal with the pressure that they are going to come under that pressure.

Not only that, but they are going to be able to step up and prove that they have the proper mental capacities to deal with the issue at hand because they will be able to find a solution rather than allow yourself to be overcome by the negative thoughts, you are going to be able to come up with solutions that are going to solve the problems that you are dealing with.

6. Commitment will come out in someone who is mentally tough because they are going to be focused on what they are trying to achieve.

   They are not going to allow anything to distract them from doing what it is that they are wanting to do, therefore they are going to be fully committed to whatever it is that they are trying to do.

7. Preparation is going to be something that mentally tough people do due to the fact that they are going to want to try and prepare for any situation that they may face.

   They are going to have solutions for all of these potiental problems because they are going to want to make sure that they are not caught off guard whenever something does come up.

8. If you are mentally tough, you are going to have motivation to reach your goals so that you are able to push yourself to get to what it is that you are wanting to achieve.

   It does not matter what you are trying to achieve, you are going to want to have motivation so that you are not just trying to get to your goal by flying by the seat of your pants.

This is going to go hand in hand with being prepared.

9. Your intensity is going come from how bad you are wanting to reach your goals.

   Athletes are going to show a massive amount of intensity due to the fact that they are going to be working to keep their fans happy and win their games.

   People in the military are going to be some of the ones who show high levels of intensity as well.

   However, there are different levels of intensity depending on what someone is trying to achieve.

   No matter what they are doing, they are going to be showing some level of intensity.

10. Those who are mentally tough are going to be able to perform under pressure.

    You are going to notice who is mentally tough and who is not by how they react under pressure.

    If you are able to stay calm and not allow the pressure to get to you, then you are going to be able to show just how mentally tough you truly are.

There are plenty of other qualities that someone who is mentally tough are going to have, however they are going to mainly show most of these qualities if not all of them.

The biggest way that you are going to know if someone is mentally tough is to see how they react under pressure as well as how they are going to react in leadership positions.

Some of the people that you are going to easily be able to notice are mentally tough are those who are or were in the military as well as athletes who are sucessful and even the business men who are high up in their company.

But, these are not the only people who are going to be the ones who are mentally tough due to the fact that even the lowest person on the totem pole is going to be able to be mentally tough.

Do not discredit someone who does not show every quality of someone who is mentally tough because some people who are just developing their mental toughness are going to be displaying a few qualities.

Chapter eleven: Steps to Building Mental Toughness

As you have learned in this book, mental toughness is going to be something that you develop therefore you are going to have steps that you are going to follow in order to build that mental toughness.

Thankfully, building mental toughness is not going to come in a few easy steps.

One of the most important things to remember is that you need to get comfortable being uncomfortable.

Not allowing yourself to stay inside of your comfort zone is going to make it to where you are able to build your mental toughness easier.

Mental toughness is not going to come to you overnight nor is it going to inspire you one day and be gone the next. It is something that you are going to have to work at and build every day.

1. Wake up early to start your day

It does not matter what you are getting up to do, get up to do it.

Everyone knows how difficult it is to get out of bed when you are comfortable at an ungodly hour, however, it is something that is going to shock your body and force you into a new routine.

You will be building mental toughness each day that you get up early and the longer that you get up to do what it is that you have to do.

The earlier in life that you start this, the easier it is going to be to continue this as you get older. However, you are never to old to start even if you feel like you are.

2. Learn something new

Go somewhere new or meet someone new.

It is going to make you uncomfortable to do this, but you have to push past this discomfort and keep your world open to the new possibilites that are going to come from you being open and allowing yourself to bring new things into your life.

It does not matter if you are trying something new or going to a new place.

The new chapter in your life that starts with these new things is typically going to mean that the previous chapter closed.

Do not be afraid to turn the page because every page that you turn is going to help you build more mental toughness than you had the day before.

3. Move towards your goal

Moving is going to help you build mental toughness.

People tend to get comfortable staying in the place that they currently are in and they are going to do next to nothing to accomplish what they are wanting as long as it is inside of their comfort zone.

But, it is going to take guts and grit to move forward and move towards the goal that pulls you out of your comfort zone.

It does not matter how big or little your goal is or if it is going to change your life or not.

Simply moving towards this goal is going to make it to where you do not stay idle because when you stay idle, you allow yourself to get comfortable and your mental toughness will begin to diminish.

4. New environments

This is going to be more for those who are in the military or are constantly moving due to their job, but you are going to be placed into situations and environments that are going to make you uncomfortable, but it is going to be part of your job.

You will have to get over your fears of things such as heights or water so that you can build your confidence and your mental toughness.

As a normal everyday person, you are going to be able to do this as well.

If you are scared of heights, work towards being able to overcome this.

If you are scared of the water, start going to small bodies of water until you overcome your fear.

The more confidence that you have, the more mental toughness you are going to have.

5. Find some way to get comfortable

While you are pulling yourself out of your comfort zone, you are going to have to find new ways to be comfortable without allowing yourself to become stagnant.

You should always chase your goals and watch as your confidence and mental toughness soar despite the fact that you are going to find yourself being uncomfortable.

Do not forget that building mental toughness is going to be something that you are going to have to work at every day or else you are going to find yourself becoming idle and once that happens, you are going to slowly slip into a life where you are not going to be comfortable.

Therefore, do not allow this to happen!

Chapter twelve: Mental Toughness and Abuse

People who have suffered from abuse are usually going to show mental toughness due to the fact that they have had to survive something that others have not had to survive.

There are all sorts of abuse out there.

Someone who is a survivor of abuse are going to be pulled out of their comfort zone by their abuser and many of them have the goal of getting away from their abuser and living a normal life.

While this does not happen for everyone who is a victim of abuse, it is easy to see how this goal is going to be able to assist someone who is able to get out of their situation.

Mental toughness is going to keep someone who has been abused going so that they are able to make it to the next day in order to see if things get better.

Whenever someone gets out of their abusive situation, they learn that they are a lot tougher than they ever thought that they were able to be due to the fact that they accomplished their biggest goal.

Someone who has been abused and is mentally tough is going to learn that they are able to keep going even when they do not feel like they are able to.

As the survivor of mental and emotional abuse, I can personally tell you that I have noticed just how mentally tough I am as I go about actually admitting to what has happened to me.

I always thought that it was my fault as to what happened to me. Not only that, but I thought that I deserved it due to the fact that I was not all that this person expected me to be.

Now, I can stand up and say that I am able to move forward and not worry about what others think about me because I was able to get myself out of the abusive situation and by being focused and committed to getting out, I was able to follow through on my goal.

Those who have been abused may not realize it, but you are tough and you are going to be able to get through it.

Do not be afraid to reach out to someone for help!

Chapter thirteen: Tips for Mentally Tough People

These tips are going to make it easier for you to build your mental toughness and build good habits that are going to make every aspect of your life easier.

1. Emotional stability: as a leader you are going to need to be able to make decisions while the pressure is mounting and piling up on you.

    You are going to need to remain objective and deliver the same performance level across the board no matter what you are feeling.

2. Perspective: your mental toughness will enable you to keep going even when it appears that everyone and everything is against you.

    You are going to be able to keep your troubles in perspective and not forget what you are trying to accomplish.

3. Ready for change: things can change in a heartbeat, so you are going to need to be flexible and adapt to the situation whenever it changes no matter when it changes or how it changes.

4. Detachment: you will have things that are going to set you back, but you need to take it in stride so that you are can come out stronger.

   The set back is not going to be because of you or about you, therefore, you should not take things personally or waste time trying to figure out why it happened.

   Instead try and focus on the things that you are able to control.

5. Strength under stress: you need to hold your resilience up whenever you find that you are facing negative situations so that you can show the world tha no matter how stressful the situation, you are going to come out on top.

6. Prepare for challenges: things are not always going to go how you want them to go, but, can make plans for these challenges that may arise so that you can face them head on without allowing them to overcome you and bring you down.

7. Focus: keep your attention on your goals and the outcomes instead of letting the obstacles pull your attention in a different direction.

8. Have the right attitude: if you allow setbacks to give you a negative attitude then you are going to be taking that attitude and losing your focus, instead you need to accept the set back and move on.

9. Self validation: you should not constantly try and please others, you will either keep them happy or upset them.

You should focus on what is the right thing to do instead of focusing on keeping others happy.

You are doing it for you, not for everyone else in the world.

10. Patience: things are not going to happen right away, and if you rush things then you are not going to get the outcome that you want.

    So, keep waiting and working hard to get to what you want so that you can get the full benefit of what it is that you are wanting to accomplish rather than rushing it and possibly being unhappy with the results.

11. Control: you are only in control of how you react to things and you need to be able to keep your emotions in check so that you do not let them overtake you and pull you down as you are trying to rise.

12. Acceptance: since you cannot control everything, you are going to need to learn that you have to accept things that you cannot control and move on from those things.

    If something happens that you are not happy with, the only thing that you are going to be able to do is accept it and move on with a new plan.

13. Endure even when you fail: Failures do not need to stop you in what you are trying to do. Instead, you should take that failure and look at it as a way for you to grow and improve rather than to give up.

    You need to keep trying until you get it the way that you want it.

If some of the most famous inventors in our history had given up, then we would not have the society that we have today.

14. Unwavering positivity: you need to stay positive even when negativity is thrown in your face.

   Do not bring yourself down to their level or allow them to bring you down because then you are not going to be able to keep moving forward with your goals.

   Staying positive is also going to make your mental health better because you are going to be fighting depression.

15. Contentment: you cannot have everything that everyone else has, thus, you should be thankful for what you have.

   If you are constantly looking at someone else and wanting what it is that they have, then you are never going to be able to achieve your goals.

   It is not a bad thing to want nice things or something that someone else has, but it should not consume you.

   You need to be happy with what you have so that you are not stopping on your path to sucess.

16. Tenacity: do not give up. Once you give up, you fail.

17. Strong inner compass: you need to know what direction you are going and do not worry about getting lost due to the fact that your internal compass is going to keep you on the right path.

Just make sure that you are staying true to yourself.

18. Uncompromising standards: do not stoop to someone else's level, keep your standards high and keep reaching for the stars.

Someone who is mentally strong is going to practice each and every day and they are going to be mindful of themselves and others.

You are going to learn from your bad habits and you are going to take those bad habits and turn them into good habits that are going to be best for you in achieving your goals.

Sometimes it is going to be hard, but there are going to be times that it is as simple as getting out of your own way and allowing things to unfold as they are meant to.

Conclusion

Thank you for making it through to the end of *Mental Toughness*, let's hope it was informative and able to provide you with all the tools you need to achieve your goals whatever it may be.

The next step is to begin to develop your mental toughness and make it to where you are able to be mentally tough no matter what situation you are placed in.

Being mentally tough is going to improve your mental health as well as make it to where you are going to be able to face difficult situations easier than most people.

Keep in mind that your mental toughness is not going to be based on genes, it is going to be based on how you develop your mental toughness.

It does not matter who you are, you can develop mental toughness!

Finally, if you found this book useful in any way, a review on Amazon is always appreciated!

Thank you and good luck!

Intermittent Fasting

Lose Fat, Build Muscle, and Get Fit

Table of Contents

reader will render any resulting actions solely under their purview.

There are no scenarios in which the publisher or the original author of this work can be in any fashion deemed liable for any hardship or damages that may befall them after undertaking information described herein.

Additionally, the information found on the following pages is intended for informational purposes only and should thus be considered, universal.

As befitting its nature, the information presented is without assurance regarding its continued validity or interim quality.

Trademarks that mentioned are done without written consent and can in no way be considered an endorsement from the trademark holder.

Introduction

Congratulations on downloading your copy of *Intermittent Fasting: Lose Fat, Build Muscle, and Get Fit.* Thank you for doing so.

Intermittent fasting has grown in popularity in recent years, thanks in large part to its ability to promote greater rates of nutrient absorption in the meals you eat.

It has also grown in popularity because it doesn't require adherents to change radically the types of foods you are eating, when you are eating, or even drastically alter the number of calories you consume in each 24-hour period.

In fact, the most common type of intermittent fasting is to simply consume two slightly larger than average meals during a day instead of the usual three.

This makes the intermittent fasting diet plan an ideal choice for those who find they have difficulty sticking to more stringent diet plans, as it only requires changing one habit, the number of meals per day, instead of many habits all at once.

Many people find that practicing intermittent fasting leads to real results.

It's simple enough to manage successfully over a prolonged period while at the same time being efficient enough to provide the type of results that can keep motivation levels high enough once the novelty of the new diet begins to fade.

The secret to intermittent fasting's success is the simple fact that your body behaves differently when it's in a fasting, versus a fed state.

When your body is in what is known as a fed state, it is actively digesting and absorbing food.

This begins some five minutes after you have finished putting food into your body, and can last anywhere from three to five hours depending on the how complicated the food is for your body to digest.

While in the fed state, your body is actively producing insulin which in turn makes it harder for it to burn fat properly.

The period after digestion has occurred, the insulin levels start dropping back towards normal which can take anywhere from 8 to 12 hours, and is the buffer between the fed and fasted state.

Once your insulin levels return to normal, the fasted state begins which is the period where your body can process fat most effectively.

Unfortunately, this means that many people never reach the point where they can burn fat most efficiently, as they rarely go eight hours, much less 12 hours from some type of caloric consumption.

There is hope! However, as to start seeing real results, all you need to do is break the three meal a day habit.

There are plenty of books on this subject on the market.

Thanks again for choosing this one.

Every effort was made to ensure it is full of as much useful information as possible.

Please enjoy!

Chapter 1: How Intermittent Fasting Works

History of Intermittent Fasting

Fasting is not a trend and has been a part of some religious beliefs including Buddhism, Islam, and Christianity.

Decades before this generation, the process may have been because of the unavailability of food resources.

Just remember, it is not a starvation diet since starvation is considered an involuntary absence of food.

Consider breakfast which is the most important time of your day. After all, it is 'break-fast'—which is a part of every day.

Fasting dates to the day of Hippocrates of Cos {c460 – c370BC} who is considered in many ideals as the father of modern medicine.

He stated, "To eat when you are sick is to feed your illness."

Plato, an ancient Greek thinker, and Aristotle, his student, were believers and supporters of fasting.

The Greeks believed that fasting is the "physician within."

This is the same logic/instinct portrayed by your pets.

Ben Franklin, an important founding father of America, also stated, "The best of all medicine is resting and fasting."

The Basics

Intermittent fasting is a way of eating to ensure that you get the most out of every meal you eat.

The core tenants of intermittent fasting mean that you don't need to change what you are eating.

Instead, you must change when you are eating it.

Intermittent fasting is a viable alternative to traditional diets or simply cutting your daily caloric intake which can help fasters lean up without changing the number of calories they consume in a day.

In fact, the preferred method of intermittent fasting is to simply eat two large meals every day instead of three (or more) meals in that same period.

Intermittent fasting is also a great option for those who traditionally have trouble sticking to diet plans since it only requires you to change one small habit, instead of several larger ones.

Intermittent fasting is extremely effective for most people because it is simple enough for them to attempt.

At the same time, it is efficient to warrant the task.

The key to understating why intermittent fasting is so successful lies in the differences in your body during a fasted state versus a fed state, as well as the important changes that will come across because of changing habits and sticking with it.

The body is considered to be in the fed state when it is in the process of absorbing and digesting food.

The fed state tends to start roughly five minutes after you begin eating, and lasting from three to five hours, depending on how long it takes your body to digest the meal.

A fed state, in turn, leads to higher levels of insulin which make it much more difficult for the body to burn fat.

The period directly after the fed sate is referred to as the post-absorptive state which is the period of time where the body is not actively processing food, and its insulin levels begin to fall.

This state lasts for between eight and twelve hours and directly precedes the fasted state.

The fasted state occurs between nine and twelve hours after the post-absorptive state and is the point where the body's insulin levels are at its lowest which in turn make it the period of time where the most fat can be burned during physical activity.

Unfortunately for many people, they rarely go twelve hours without eating which means that no matter how hard they exercise they are not burning fat as efficiently as possible.

However, this also means that you can burn fat and build muscle by simply altering your feeding habits.

Scientifically Proven

Your metabolic rate is increased with short-term fasting because of the hormonal changes ranging in categories of 3.6% to 14%.

Studies have established weight loss after three to twenty-four weeks on the intermittent fasting program to maintain losses of 3.0 to 8.0%.

In comparison to other studies on weight loss, these are high percentages that cannot be ignored.

In the same studies, many of the individuals lost 4.0 to 7.0% of his/her waist circumference.

This is an indication of how the harmful buildup of belly fat can cause disease and other issues around your organs.

You have to consider these results are from eating fewer overall calories, and not binging during the days off.

You must maintain a sensible eating program.

While the science behind intermittent fasting is certainly promising, there are a few things you will need to keep in mind when starting any new dietary plan.

No diet, regardless of how miraculous it appears, can help you if you don't obey a few golden rules:

- *Keep a calorie deficit:* While this is true for any diet, it is even more true for intermittent fasting since it can be so easy to overeat once you do eat in such a way that it negates any benefits you might have felt.

Remember, you need to burn 3,500 calories weekly to lose one pound each week.

- *Maintain self-control:* Intermittent fasting only works if your body goes completely without food for at least twelve hours and any caloric intact resets the cycle.

  As such, it is extremely important to ensure that you maintain control of you bodily urges if you hope to see real results from this type of approach.

  Remember, fasting for at least twelve hours only allows you to eat normally or slightly more than an average meal, it does not give you license to eat everything in sight.

  Keeping your appetites in check is a strict requirement for success.

- *Be consistent:* Regardless of the type of weight loss that you ultimately choose to pursue, it is important to choose one and stick with it.

  Attempting an intermittent fast for a few days before switching to another plan such as the Paleo diet before trying out a low-carb approach will only cause your body to freak out and hold on to every possible calorie until it figures out what in the world is happening.

  Remember, fasting regularly and consistently is the surest way to see any of its benefits.

  Only after your body has time to adjust to your new routine will it then be able to adapt appropriately.

It can begin to increase several positive enzymes and neural pathways to maximize weight loss using this method.

Consider consistency the ace-in-the-hole of proactive weight loss success.

Possible Side Effects:

While intermittent fasting has some scientifically proven benefits, it is not with its potential side effects.

The biggest one of these is the initial change in your bowel movements as periods of constipation or in some cases diarrhea could occur.

Fortunately, they should not last more than a few days as your body adjusts to the new method of caloric intake.

Additional damage can be done to the body if periods of fasting are routinely followed by periods of excessive binging.

It is important to attempt intermittent fasting, and your periods of eating after, in moderation.

If you notice any serious immediate physical changes after you begin any form of dieting regime, it is important to consult a nutritionist.

Chapter 2: Intermittent Types and Fasting Schedules

While the core ideas behind the various forms of intermittent fasting are all the same, there are quite a few different ways to go about it.

Your best bet is to try a few and see which one your body naturally responds to the easiest.

16:8 Method

This method involves fasting for 16 hours for men, or 14 hours for women, before allowing a reasonable number of calories for the remaining 8 to 10 hours.

During this period, you should only consume items that have zero calories including black coffee (a splash of cream is fine), water, diet soda, and sugar-free gum.

The easiest way to attempt this schedule is to stop eating after dinner in the evening and wait 14 or 16 hours from there.

This means skipping breakfast and picking things up in the early afternoon.

Again, the specifics of when you fast are not nearly as important as ensuring that you fast for the same period of time as regularly as possible.

If you vary your fasting period too much, it can lead to an erratic change in your hormones, which among other things; make it much more difficult for your body to shed any excess weight.

If you find yourself without the time required to eat a proper meal to break the fast normally, ensure you at least eat something to keep your body on the correct cycle.

If you are exercising, as well as intermittently fasting, it is important to ensure that you are eating more carbohydrates than fats while you are working out, while on days you are not exercising the opposite is true.

It is important to ensure that every day you keep your protein intake at a steady level.

Stay away from processed foods whenever possible.

One of the biggest benefits of this type of fasting is that it's extremely flexible so that it will work for a wide variety schedules.

Most people find it helpful to either eat two large meals during the 8 or 10-hour period feeding period or split that time into three smaller meals as that is the way most people are already programmed.

On days you are exercising as well as fasting, it is important to try and always break your fast with a mix of protein, vegetables, and fruit.

If you generally go to the gym directly after you have broken your fast, it is important to include enough carbohydrates to give your muscles the energy they need to get the most out of your workout.

If you are planning to exercise, it is usually best to start the early afternoon healthy with a medium calorie meal.

Then, exercise within three hours before eating a larger meal soon afterward.

In this larger meal, it is important to add a larger portion of complex carbohydrates.

You can even have a little dessert as long as it is in moderation. Remember, fasting is different than dieting.

On days you do not plan on exercising, it is important to adjust your caloric intake appropriately.

Start by limiting your carbohydrate intake, and instead focus on eating lots of protein, dark green, leafy vegetables and fruit in moderation.

Unlike on days you are exercising, the first meal you eat on rest days should be your largest regarding caloric intake with this one meal counting for about 40 percent of your daily total.

Remember, during this meal, you should be taking in more protein than anything else.

For your final meal during rest days, it is important to include a protein source that will take lots of time to digest which in turn means it will keep you full for more of your fast the following morning.

It also provides the body with enough stored amino acids to prevent it from breaking down muscle during the fast.

Eat-Stop-Eat

This form of fasting can be considered the most beneficial to those who are already eating healthy but want to give their weight loss an extra boost.

On this type of program, you don't eat anything one or two days a week.

During this period, you should only consume things that have zero calories including black coffee (a splash of cream is fine), water, diet soda, and sugar-free gum.

When you are finished fasting, it is important not to eat too much more than normal and always to avoid binging as extended periods of fast/binge cycles can cause serious damage to your body.

As always, it is important to practice moderation and self-control to get the most out of the fasting cycle.

This fast cycle works on the assumption that in to lose a pound of weight a week, all you need to do is give up 3,500 calories.

So, it might be best to get it out of the way in two quick bursts rather than fasting for a portion of every single day.

This fasting plan emphasizes resistance weight training for maximum benefits.

Going a full day without eating can be difficult for some people at first, but it is perfectly acceptable to work up to a full day of fasting by holding out as long as possible and increasing that amount of time with practice.

A good way to start is by choosing days that you know don't have any prior food commitments.

Beginning a fasting program on a day when you know you have a lunch meeting is just a bad idea.

When first starting this fast cycle, fatigue, headaches or feelings of anger or anxiousness are all common side-effects and should be considered a good stopping point for your current fast.

These side-effects will diminish as your body adjusts to the new cycle.

After going a full day without any calories, it will be natural to have the desire to binge during your fist meal.

You must have the self-control to fight these urges since not only is binging bad for you; it can easily undo all your hard work from the previous 24 hours. Practice self-discipline and make your fasting worth the effort.

The Warrior Diet

The Warrior Diet takes the 16:8 Program and kicks it up a notch by recommending that you fast for roughly 20 hours out of each day followed by one meal where you get all your calories in the four remaining hours of the day.

This form of intermittent fasting follows the belief that humans are naturally nocturnal eaters.

Therefore, eating at night helps the body more easily process the nutrients it needs.

In this case, fasting is a bit of a misnomer as during the 20-hour period you are allowed to eat a serving of raw vegetables or fruits and maybe a serving of protein if you just can't otherwise continue.

This works because it causes the body's natural sympathetic nervous system to activate a flight or fight response which in turns increases your natural levels of alertness, and increases energy while at the same time increasing the amount of fat burned.

The large meal each evening then allows the body to focus on repairing itself and improving its muscles.

When following the Warrior Diet, it is important to start each evening meal with vegetables, followed by protein, fat, and carbohydrates.

This form of fasting is popular for two reasons.

First, the fact that a few small and reasonable snacks are allowed during the fasting process making this type of fasting attractive to those who are attempting the practice for the first time.

Second, nearly everyone who attempts this form of fasting reports a significant amount of increased energy throughout the day as well as increase in the amount of fat lost per week.

On the other hand, the relatively strict nature of this diet can make it difficult for some people to follow for long periods of time.

The timing of the large meal can also make it difficult for some people to follow because it can naturally interfere with some social engagements.

Finally, some people don't like having to eat their food in a specific order.

Try it for yourself and see what works for you.

Fat Loss Forever

This form of intermittent fasting combines elements of several other styles of fasting to create something rather unique.

The good news is that you get a cheat day every week.

The bad news is that it is followed by a one and a half day fast with the remainder of the week being split between 16:8 and 20:4 fasting.

For this diet, it is important to schedule your exercise rest days for the second part of the 36-hour cycle.

Otherwise, it is important to stay as busy on these days as possible to help combat your hunger.

If you find it hard to control your appetite on cheat days, then this form of intermittent fasting may not be for you since it requires you to go from sixty to zero quickly and regularly.

Also, it is important not to try and last 36 hours without eating food all at once.

You will need to build up your body's tolerance for fasting.

As such, it is usually better to start with another form of intermittent fasting and work up to the Fat Loss Forever method after your body has already gotten out of the habit of eating every three or four hours.

Remember to always fast responsibly, and never push your body to the point where you feel physically ill.

Also, remember it is important to fast on a routine to allow your body the time it needs to adjust to the change.

Alternate Day Diet

This form of intermittent fasting actually means you never have to go long without food, if you so choose.

Every other day you eat normally, and on the off-days, you simply consume one-fifth of the calories you consume on the normal days.

The average daily caloric consumption is between 2,000 and 2,500 calories which mean that the average off-day varies between 400 and 500 calories.

If you enjoy exercising every day, then this form of intermittent fasting may not be for you since you will have to severely limit your workouts on off-days.

When you first start this form of intermittent fasting, the easiest way to make it through the low-calorie days is by trying any one of a variety of protein shakes.

It is important to work back to 'real' natural foods on these days because they will always be healthier than the shakes.

This form of intermittent fasting is all about losing weight.

Those who try it tend to average between two and three pounds lost per week.

If you attempt the Alternate Day Diet, it is extremely important to eat regularly on your full-calorie days.

Binging will not only negate any progress you have made, but it can also cause serious damage to your body if continued over time.

Irregularly Skipping Meals

If you are interested in trying out the benefits of intermittent fasting for yourself, but you have an irregular schedule or are not sure if it is for you, then skipping a meal or two now and then may be the type of intermittent fasting for you.

As previously discussed, getting into a fasting routine is important to see the maximum results for your effort, but that doesn't mean occasionally fasting doesn't come with some benefits as well.

What's more, once you have tried skipping a meal now and then you can see for yourself just how easy it is which in turn can lead to more positive changes down the line.

With so many intermittent fasting options available the odds are good that one fits your schedule, so give it a try. What have you got to lose (besides a few pounds)?

Chapter 3: Health Benefits

Other than weight loss, you can receive benefits from intermittent fasting in many other ways.

You will live a longer life from achieving an extended fasting state and diverting your energy while improving your biological functions.

Just remember, the plan will not in any way cause you to starve.

The emergency signals transported by your body is simply that—a signal.

The fasting state your body is experiencing will diminish once your body adjusts to the diet method of intermittent fasting you choose to take.

These are some of the crucial elements to consider:

- *Brain Health:* Your brain hormone—BDNF—also known as brain-derived "neurotropic" factor—is a protein that can aid in the growth of new nerve cells.

  It is also believed to provide protection against Alzheimer's and Parkinson's disease.

- *Cancer:* Studies using animals have suggested intermittent fasting can be beneficial in the prevention of cancer.

- *Heart Health:* The blood triglycerides, LDL cholesterol, insulin resistance, and blood sugar can be reduced using this plan.

Each of these presents a huge risk element for heart ailments or disease.

- *Inflammation:* Chronic diseases are driven by inflammation, and the fasting plans help to reduce the inflammation as proven by private studies.

Your body will be capable of repairing, healing, and recovering more quickly than without the diet plan.

- *Insulin Resistance:* Your blood sugar levels can be lowered by 3.0% to 3.6 as fasting insulin levels can also decrease as much as 20% to 31%.

These figures indicate you should be better sheltered against type 2 diabetes as well as a more continuous level of mood and energy stages.

- *Anti-Aging:* The process has only been tested using animals, but the rats tested lived 36% to 83% longer than ones that were not fasting.

- *Lower Stress Levels:* The cortisol production is lowered.

- *Fatty Acid Oxidation:* Your body will burn more fats as energy with the oxidation process and will also provide quick weight loss.

Note: Each of these studies are in early stages.

More research needs to be provided using human testing during the fasting process.

Chapter 4: The Process

While intermittent fasting is undeniably beneficial, it can be difficult to get started or to see through to the point where your body adapts to a new schedule.

The following tips and tricks can help set you on the path to success.

Have a conversation with yourself:

Intermittent fasting has a wide variety of proven benefits, but it is not for everyone.

Before you attempt a fast, it is important to have a real dialogue with yourself.

Consider your level of self-discipline, your current attachment to food, any regular activities that would make fasting difficult or awkward, your general lifestyle, and your level of exercise.

Deciding to try a different fitness regime is a lot easier on day one, than after struggling through a week or more of faulty fasting.

Watch your response:

While it is important to keep tabs on how your body is responding to intermittent fasting, it is doubly important to monitor your vitals during the initial phase when your body is adjusting to the new feeding times.

Some discomfort is to be expected for the first three to four weeks, but anything longer or more severe should be discussed with a doctor as soon as possible.

The early days will have ups and downs:

While your body adjusts to intermittent fasting, there will be times where you are losing weight and times where your body is trying to hold on to every calorie it has.

This is natural and to be expected as your body realigns its hormone levels.

Drink lots of water:

Not only will water help you feel full throughout your fast, staying hydrated is akin to staying healthy.

Aim for at least a gallon of water per day.

Caffeine naturally suppresses the appetite:

Black coffee works best as there is little to it which can negatively affect your metabolism or general wellbeing.

The same cannot be said for most 0-calorie caffeinated beverages.

Artificial sweeteners have been shown to cause some health problems.

Still, anything with caffeine will help calm your appetite for at least a little while.

Keep yourself busy:

Ensure that the latter parts of your fast aren't just spent waiting around to eat.

Intermittent fasting has the possibility to be either extremely difficult or surprisingly easy depending solely on how much of the time you spend thinking about food.

Find ways to occupy your mind, and you will be surprised how quickly meal time will roll around.

Start each fast off right:

At the start of your fast, your body will still have the most fuel in its system to work with, which is why it is best to start each fast with the most difficult items on your to-do list.

As you move farther and farther from the last period of time, and you take in fresh calories, your thought processes will naturally begin to slow in your body's effort to save energy.

Difficult tasks will inherently seem easier when your body is working at maximum efficiency.

Make it work for you:

Intermittent fasting can work around any type of schedule which is part of what makes it so great.

If you find yourself feeling trapped by the period of time you are allowing yourself to eat, why don't you move it?

Fasting should be about adding freedom to your schedule, not restraining it.

Don't expect results overnight:

As previously discussed, it will take some time for your body to adjust fully to your new dietary patterns, and for it to start reflecting these new results.
Try intermittent fasting regularly for at least a month before rendering judgment on the success of the plan.

Vary your schedule:

After you have given your body time to adjust to an intermittent fasting schedule, it is important to take the time to fluctuate your on/off patterns throughout the day to see what works best for you.

Taking the time to experiment may yield unexpected results.

Start slow:

If you find that you are having difficulty starting the transition to an intermittent fasting program full bore, try moving your breakfast time back one hour each week.

Before you know it, you will have reached a 16:8 or 14:10 split without even trying.

Keep it to yourself:

While there is plenty of scientific evidence that supports intermittent fasting, there are still plenty of skeptics out there.

That negativity isn't something you need, especially when you are first starting out.

After you have started seeing results for yourself, it will be much easier to defend the process to non-believers.

Just show them a before and after picture.

Start the day off with a belly full of liquid:

Often the signals for hunger and the signals for thirst can get crossed in your brain.

After it has sent out enough ignored thirst signals, it starts sending out hunger signals instead.

As such, starting the morning off by drinking at least half a liter of water is an excellent way to quench your body's thirst from the past seven or eight hours.

It should be enough to keep you feeling full for at least a few extra hours each morning.

Don't take on too much, too fast:

Even if you think you feel fine when you first begin an intermittent fast cycle, it is important to always give your body the time it needs to recover.

Never go more than two days out of a week without eating.

There is an important distinction between fasting and starving yourself.

Splurge when you want:

Remember that you need to burn 3,500 calories to lose a pound a week, but how you do that is up to you.

If you want to have a particularly appetizing dessert or unhealthy main course, that is perfectly fine, as long as you make an effort to make up the difference throughout the week.

Distract yourself:

Distraction is especially important as your body is adapting to your new eating habits, and becomes increasingly important the farther into a fast you go.

Try going out and being active when you are struggling with the plan to help refocus your thinking patterns.

Besides, the exercise also helps push away the pounds.

Add protein to your meals:

There is nothing better at combating hunger than protein, plain and simple.

It is also great for building lean muscle.

If you find yourself unable to get through even 10 hours without eating, then it might be a sign that you should add more protein to your diet.

Try Branched Chain Amino Acids:

For those on a low-calorie diet such as intermittent fasting, studies show that a BCAA supplement will stimulate additional fat loss while at the same time preventing lean muscle from being consumed as the body tries to feed itself.

Intermittent fasting is not an excuse to eat poorly:

Intermittent fasting works on the principle that eating fewer calories than you burn is a surefire way to lose weight.

This theory falls apart if you use the fact that you are fasting as an excuse to eat nothing but junk food when you are eating.

Self-control and self-discipline are both equally important when it comes to eating properly. Intermittent fasting has a wide variety of health benefits.

Why not accentuate them even more with a healthy diet to go along with it?

Break your fast the right way:

The content and quality of your first meal of the day can easily set the tone for those that follow.

Use this to your advantage, and start your feeding window off right with something fit and healthy.

You will be surprised at how much this improves your willpower for later meals.

Consider the difference between head hunger and body hunger:

As you get used to the process of intermittent fasting, you will become acquainted with several different types of hunger and ultimately learn how to tell when you are truly hungry as opposed to just habitually used to eating.

While it will initially be difficult to tell the difference, you will come to know them both intimately in time.

Learn what your body is saying:

While many people consider a sudden craving for a particular type of food as an indication that they are hungry, and take action to respond accordingly.

This, in fact, is often just a craving brought on by an ancient part of the brain which equates things that are salty, sweet, and high in fat as vital parts of a regular diet.

Since once upon a time, having those three qualities equated to things that were high in positive nutrients as well.

This is no longer the case and tends to be the opposite these days.

As such, these types of urges can safely be ignored.

Take the time to investigate a sudden surge of hunger to see if it could instead be related to your emotional state instead of your physical one.

Exercise in moderation:

Dieting works by ensuring that you are taking in fewer calories than you are burning in a fixed period of time.

As such, if you are trying one of the intermittent fasting options that involve you not eating for a day or more, then it is extremely important to ensure that you adjust your exercise plan for these days as well.

When exercising, your body requires fuel. It will take it from your muscles if you don't give it another choice.

Exercising too much while you're fasting is a guaranteed recipe for disaster.

Don't cover real issues with fasting:

Those with a penchant for eating disorders or those who believe they might be should stay away for intermittent fasting as it can easily lead to more serious issues if not controlled properly.

Remember, it is important to have the willpower to stop eating for a set period of time, but it is also equally important to have the willpower to begin eating again once the fast is over.

Chapter 5: Weight Loss and Intermittent Fasting

You need to understand what your daily calorie needs will be to adopt a realistic diet plan and maintain a new desirable weight.

The use of an adult BMI and Calorie Calculator will be an essential tool if the calories are not indicated in the recipe.

Most products you purchase will have ingredient panels listing the counts, so you will have a general idea of how to plan your menu around your intermittent fasting plan.

You will need to enter your sex, height, weight, and age into the calculator.

You will also need to provide the calculator with your daily activity schedule (such as daily—more than an hour—less than an hour—or rarely.

The BMI will indicate your BMI score and the amount of calories necessary to maintain your current body weight.

It will make your goals simpler to map by providing you with the tallies from your calculations to lower your counts.

Maintain a Healthy Diet Plan

The components for a healthier eating pattern using intermittent fasting methods will account for all the beverages and foods within a suitable calorie level.

A good plan for a healthy fasting pattern will include the following:

- Whole Fruits
- Oils
- Grains (a minimum of half should be whole grains)
- Protein foods such as eggs, poultry, lean meats, seafood, nuts, seeds, and soy products
- Varied veggies from all the main subgroups include— starchy legumes (peas and beans), red and orange, dark green and others.

Health concerns in the United States are focused on fundamental elements that should be limited when using the intermittent fasting diet plan.

They recommend you do the following:

- Consume less than 10% of your daily calories from saturated fats.
- Eat less than 10% of your daily intake of calories from added sugars.
- Sodium consumption should be less than 2,300 mg (milligrams).
- Moderation must be accompanied if you consume alcohol products.

You should have no more than one daily if you are a woman and only two each day if you are a man.

What Not to Eat

With all the talk of the importance of natural foods, what foods should I avoid to make my intermittent fast more effective?

As a general rule, the following foods should be avoided or at least limited as much as possible.

- *Processed Meats:* While protein is an undeniably important part of a healthy diet, seeking your protein from meats which have been processed will stuff your body so full of chemicals that any benefits the meal might have had are otherwise lost.

  These meats tend to be lower in protein while higher in sodium and preservatives that can cause a variety of health risks, including asthma and heart disease, than the quality of the cuts of meat found in most grocery stores.

- *Non-organic potatoes:* While starch and the carbohydrates they contain are an important part of a balanced meal, non-organic potatoes are not worth the trouble.

  They are treated with chemicals while still in the ground.

  They are treated again before they head to the store to ensure they stay "fresh" as long as possible.

  These chemicals have been shown to increase the risk of health issues like autism, asthma, birth defects, learning disabilities, Parkinson's and Alzheimer's disease as well as multiple types of cancer.

- *Farm-raised salmon:* Much like processed meat, farm-raised salmon are the least healthy type of an otherwise healthy meal choice.

  When salmon are raised in tubs near one another for a prolonged period of time, they lose much of their natural vitamin D while picking up traces of PCB, DDT, carcinogens, and bromine.

  Choose wild caught fish if possible.

- *Non-organic milk:* Despite being touted as part of a balanced diet, non-organic milk is routinely found to be full of growth hormones as well as puss as a result of over-milking the cows.

  The growth hormones leave behind antibiotics which can, in turn, make it more difficult for the human body to counter infections as well as causing an increased chance of colon cancer, prostate cancer, and breast cancer.

- *White Flour:* Much like processed meats, by the time white flour is done being produced; it is completely devoid of any nutritional value.

  When eaten as part of a regular diet, white flour has been shown to increase a woman's chance of breast cancer by a shocking 200 percent.

These are just a few of the reasons that processed foods should be considered a problem in the modern world.

Processed foods can be considered any items which contain preservatives, chemical colors, flavorings, additives or chemicals which change its texture.

An additional extremely important warning sign of unhealthy food is when an item contains a large amount of carbohydrates in their refined form.

The cliff-notes version is this, the sooner you begin to take the time to read labels and check ingredients, the sooner you can start getting the most out of the meals you eat in between intermittent fasting sessions. Making a real, consciousness effort to do so may very well be the difference between life and death.

Chapter 6: Intermittent Fasting and Nutrition

How to Boost Your Metabolism

With all the hard work for your intermittent fasting, it is always good to know there are other ways to speed up the process at the same time.

It is good to know these are some of the specific foods you should eat to help the metabolism process of losing weight:

Protein-Rich Food Groups

Your body will need more energy to digest these products:

- Eggs

- Seeds and nuts

- Legumes

- Fish

- Meat

- Fish

The thermic effect of food is referred to as TEF which is the number of calories required by your body to absorb/digest the nutrients received by your meals.

The protein intake will also make you have a full feeling much longer, and possibly prevent you from overeating.

Essential Vitamins and Minerals

Zinc, iron, and selenium are essential for your healthy body functions.

It is shown by research a diet low in these elements reduces the ability of the thyroid gland to produce crucial hormones.

This process will significantly slow the metabolism down.

It is best to eat seeds, nuts, legumes, meat, and seafood.

- *Chili Peppers:* The chemical found in chili peppers is called capsaicin which will boost your metabolism.

  The capsaicin will increase the fat and calories you burn during your intermittent fasting plan.

  Twenty research studies indicated you would lose/burn approximately fifty extra calories daily.

  However, now all researchers agree with the theory.

  At any rate, enjoy the chili peppers.

- *Pulses and Legumes:* This food group includes peanuts, lentils, chickpeas, beans, and peas which are extremely high in protein levels in comparison to other plant foods.

  According to research studies, your higher protein counts will require your body to burn a larger number of calories to digest them, versus the lower-protein foods.

Recent studies have indicated participants who consumed a legume-rich diet for eight weeks increased the metabolism rate and lost more than 1.5 times more weight versus the other controlled group of applicants.

- *Coffee:* Your caffeine levels can help increase the metabolic rate by approximately 11%.

  Studies have shown consumption of a minimum of 270 mg of caffeine—about three cups of coffee—will burn away an additional 100 calories daily.

  The rates can surely boost your intermittent fasting as long as you leave it sugar-free.

- *Tea:* Tea is offered as a good source of beverage because of the catechins in the tea conglomerate with the caffeine to help speed up your metabolism.

  The catechins are an antioxidant and a type of natural phenol which is from the chemical family of flavonoids.

  An additional 100 calories can be burned daily to increase your metabolism by four to ten percent with the use of green and oolong tea.

  The effects may be different with each fasting participant.

Chapter 7: Different Methods for Everyday Living

Method 16:8 or the Lean Gains Diet Plan

Another term for this plan is the Lean Gains protocol which implicates for a time slot of eight hours that you can eat a restricted diet and fast for the remainder time of sixteen hours for men and fourteen hours for women.

Hugh Jackman was the emblem used to discover the facts and make the headlines.

The 16:8 method for intermittent fasting is the most preferred method for weight loss—besides you will be sleeping for approximately eight of those fasting hours.

On the remainder eight to ten hours, the meals should be slightly larger while still relatively health conscious.

The fasting period allows for zero calorie consumption.

If you are overweight and have a sedentary lifestyle; you should avoid most of the starchy carbohydrates.

You have to cram all of your calories in that time allotment to ensure the successes of the plan.

Many individuals on the plan can fit two filling meals into the eight to ten-hour time frame or three regular meals if desired.

Once again, the most important element is consistency.

A study was performed by the Obesity Society stating if you have your dinner before 2:00 p.m., your hunger yearnings will be reduced for the remainder of the day.

At the same time, your fat-burning reserves are boosted.

No matter what you have heard about this plan, you will not be as hungry once you have the plan and your menu scheduled.

That is the secret to a slimmer body, get the counts right.

Another advantage is that you can begin the plate at any time that suits your schedule.

You can use these sample menus as a basis for your plan:

Day 1

- **Morning:** Tea, water, or coffee is allowed with a small amount of milk or heavy cream

- **Lunch:** Chicken Breast/black bean sauce, green veggies, and fruit.

- **Dinner:** Salmon and baked veggies with one potato. (If this is too much for one meal, break it in half and eat it later.

Day 2: Repeat Day 1

Additional Tips

- *Sugar Substitutes:* Xylitol can replace sugar. Replace the coffee with black or green tea (advisable if you like the tastes).

- *Stay Hydrated:* Drink plenty of tea, water, or coffee during the morning hours. It also helps prevent the pangs of hunger you will feel. If possible, replace the coffee with black or green tea.

- *Sleep:* You need to have a full eight hours of sleep. It is advisable to avoid your cell phone and laptop (blue light) for up to an hour before you are ready to retire for the evening.

The Consistent Path

The goal is to set your eating schedule to the same time daily to program our body.

If you vary during the fasting plan, your hormones will be all over the place, resulting in your body holding onto the weight instead of detaching from the extra pounds.

It is also important to keep your protein on an even kilter throughout your fasting schedule.

For women, it should remain at 55 grams daily.

For men, it should be in the area of 60 grams daily.

If you consume the correct levels of protein and exercise regularly while taking in a steady amount of carbs, you should have all the energy needed on a daily basis.

However, if you are less inclined to exercise you should focus on healthy fats while you minimize the carbs.

Aim for approximately 0.7 grams of healthy fats for each pound of body weight daily.

As with the other plans, it is best to avoid processed foods and unhealthy fats while searching for healthier—natural alternatives when possible.

If you are not an avid exerciser, you also need to adjust your meals for the days to ensure you don't overeat accidentally.

Eat-Stop-Eat

Once or twice each week, you will fast for twenty-four hours.

As an illustration, you would eat dinner one morning and not eat again until the following morning.

Most professionals say if you make it to twenty hours; it's okay.

To further condition your body, for two days eat about 2,500 calories if you are a man and 2,000 if you are a woman.

After several regular eating days, attempt another fasting, and repeat the agenda.

Non-Fasting and Fasting Day Nutrients

For the days on an active fast, try not to consume many calories.

You can drink sparkling or plain water, diet soda, coffee, or tea.

When the fast is complete, eat what you like using restraint.

Enjoy plenty of veggies, fruits, and take advantage of the spices for variety.

Protein should be apparent using twenty to thirty grams of high-quality protein.

Consume a total of one-hundred grams every four to five hours.

You can use protein powders if needed.

If you are gaining extra pounds in between your fasting schedule, consider cutting back by approximately 10% on the amount of food you consume on non-fasting days.

Some individuals cannot 'hack' the plan and state it makes him/her less adaptable to enjoying time with friends at social gatherings.

Many have issues of crankiness and headaches which can lead to the plan's failure.

With that said, the plan's benefits are overwhelming because you can judge your progress, and you choose to eat.

It takes learning some self-control, but you can get it.

Note: Never fast two consecutive days. Also, you should not take the challenge more than two fasting days in one week.

Fluid Intake

With a strict plan such as this one, you must remain hydrated.

You can drink plenty of clear liquids, but where are the nutrients?

On your fasting days, stick to apple juice, water, broth, cranberry juice, ice pops, plain gelatin, black coffee or tea.

This is okay since you will be fasting for twenty to twenty-four hours.

You can also enjoy foods including ice cream, skim milk, juice with pulp, or strained creamy soup.

Try a whey protein supplemental shake or some low-fat frozen yogurt.

These choices will provide some essential nutrients, fiber, as well as the necessary calorie counts.

Just be sure to use low-calorie juices, ice cream, and a few ice cubes for a smoothie treat.

It is advisable to confer with your physician before you begin this or any other dieting plan.

While you are fasting, you might need to discontinue any dietary supplements or medications.

According to research at Vanderbilt University, daily liquid diets will provide you between 400 to 800 calories.

Additional Tips

With this fasting method, it is essential to not fall into a habit of fasting and binging because it will create havoc within your body.

It is more than your body can handle since the cycle will only work for individuals who can practice control and moderate consumption of food.

It is recommended by the professionals to perform resistance-style weight training on the days you aren't fasting.

Try a minimal yoga session or light cardio exercise if you feel completely out of it on your fasting days.

Any more vigorous exercising could make it difficult to achieve the time allotment of your fasting schedule.

Remember, at first—it is common to feel angered, anxious, fatigued, or have headaches.

This will pass once your body adjusts to the new dieting plan.

Try to keep in mind that every single day you can successfully stay on your desired plan is one more day toward your successful goal.

The Warrior Diet

It is believed that the name of the diet is a reflection of the ancient ancestors who were natural nocturnal eaters.

As a step up from the Lean Gains diet and as a variation of the daily fast; the Warrior Diet is a plan promoting one healthy meal daily—usually dinner.

The method is parallel with the human 24-hour rhythm and can encourage excellent general health while removing the harmful toxins from your body.

You should try to eat at least several hours before going to sleep for the night.

The Daytime Feeding Schedule

For the plan to be effective, you need to consume less food during the daytime hours.

Eat small servings of veggies, fruits, and a protein such as a yogurt, whey protein, or kefir.

Sidestep consumption of meats, grains, refined foods (pasta, corn tortillas, etc.) which lack the nutrient and are usually processed foods. Also, avoid sugary beverages and treats.

Every few hours, you should eat a small serving of protein or fruit.

Eat green veggies such as celery, leafy greens, cucumbers, and peppers which are not restricted to your intake amounts.

Nighttime Feeding Frenzy

You can eat as much food as you wish but keep the correct food combinations. Enlist as many different aromas, colors, and textures to create new taste sensations for your evening meal.

Eliminate or avoid using white vinegar.

When you feel full or have satisfied your hunger or if you become more thirsty than hungry; it is time to stop eating.

Follow the Rules

Start off with your salad, protein, and veggies and complete the meal with a few fats or carbs.

Take a short twenty-minute break after the protein and vegetables which will be a signal to your brain to recharge your appetite.

If you are still hungry, continue your meal.

Organic foods are the best choices which will include grass-fed, free range, and hormone free animal products.

Your eggs, dairy, and meat, as well as your fish consumption, should be a 'wild' catch.

Processed sugars are considered toxic on this diet plan.

You should also exercise as a critical step in your fasting plan.

After your workout, consume 20 to 30 grams of net protein with no additional sugar.

Guidelines for Success

Remember to plan your menus ahead of time to be sure you have the right combination of foods.

Vegetables and protein will combine with your entire menu planning needs. Starch, sugar, and fat cannot conglomerate effectively.

Examples of the Right Combinations

- Eggs and beans

- Seeds and nuts

- Eggs and potatoes

- Berries and Whey protein

- Cocoa nibs and peanut butter

- Potatoes and peas

- Nuts and wine

- Cheese and wine

- Rice and beans

Examples of the Wrong Combinations

- Pasta and wine

- Pasta and nuts

- Raisins and nuts (trail mix)

- Sugar and cream

- Jelly and peanut butter

- Jam and bread

- Granola (honey nut)

- Sour cream and potatoes

Sample Plan: Daytime Options

Early Morning: Tea, coffee, or cacao (no sugar) whole milk

Mid-morning: Vegetable juice or one fruit (8 ounces of berries)

Lunchtime: Salad with tomatoes, peppers, mixed greens, mushroom, onions, sprouts, and cucumber

Dressing for the salad: Use a small amount of olive oil OR whey protein

Afternoon: Fresh Fruit or Vegetable juice

Sample Plan: Nighttime Meal

For your one large meal of the day try some of the following food groups:

Protein: Eggs (cooked or poached), wild catch fish, organic cheeses such as goat and cottage

Cooked Veggies: Grilled or steamed cauliflower, broccoli, zucchini, onion, spinach, okra, and mushroom

Raw Veggies: Broccoli sprouts, salad greens, as well as red, yellow, and orange vegetables

Carbs: Use puree from butternut squash, carrots, Brussels sprouts, turnips, pumpkin, or cauliflower (steamed rooted veggies)

Use modest amounts of aged cheese, olive paste, parmesan cheese, or goat feta to top off your protein and vegetables.

During the detox meals, you can also reduce stress with green tea and berberine.

The berberine is a supplement to help unlock your metabolism to help balance your blood sugar levels during the detox diet plan.

The warrior diet is one of the most popular plans because it allows a sensible number of snacks to the daily routine which makes it more appealing to beginners on the fasting path.

The amount of energy will naturally get your body in the habit of burning fat for fuel.

Every-Other-Day Diet Plan

The alternate days using this plan was established by an assistant professor, Dr. Krista Varady, from the University of Illinois.

Women should consume between 500 to 600 calories, and men need to consume more than 400 to 500 calories daily.

However, on the feast day, you can eat anything you want and as much as you want.

The plan takes some planning since the diet begins between the hours of noon and 2 pm. These are some of the items to make your day more enjoyable:

The following meal will supply you with roughly 475 calories—depending on the type of soup used.

- ½ cup cooked chicken cooked without the skin and topped/Lemon juice/Fresh-ground pepper

- Bowl of tomato or low-sodium vegetable soup

- 1 ¼ cups of fruit salad

For Men Only: You can have a whole-wheat roll (medium 96-calorie) for a total of 566 calories.

Prepare the salad with pears strawberries, mandarin orange segments, and melon.

Enjoy Lean Beef
Choose a lean piece of beef cut similar to sirloin or tenderloin steak, and enjoy some low-calorie side dishes.

The basics of the plan are calculated for women.

For men, add 80 additional calories with a one-cup serving of asparagus with a teaspoon of olive oil for the topping.

For the remainder of the meal, enjoy a three-ounce seared steak with some onions.

Top it off with a bit of blue cheese.

Serve it with one cup of chard sautéed in 1 teaspoon of olive oil along with a ½ cup of polenta (cornmeal).

Use some lemon juice for seasoning.

Substitute with Seafood:
You need to consume some omega-3 fatty acids to remain heart-healthy.

For men, boost the counts to 553 by enjoying one cup of kale that has been sautéed with olive oil for an additional 102 calories.

Flavor the kale with crushed red pepper, red wine vinegar, and garlic.

For a woman (451 calories) enjoy three ounces of sautéed shrimp with jalapenos, garlic, onions, and some tomatoes (fresh and diced) on a bed of ½ cup of brown rice.

Place it all in a six-inch corn tortilla.

Also, have ¼ of an avocado (chopped) for dessert.

The Choice of No Meat:
Women can choose a meatless meal with 473 calories using a whole-wheat pizza crust.

As toppings use some black beans, diced tomatoes, barbecue sauce, fresh corn, and shredded mozzarella cheese.

Have a bowl of butternut squash soup, made using ¾ cup of fruit sorbet and veggie stock.

Men can veg-out with one cup of cauliflower salad for an extra 48 calories using reduced-fat mayonnaise.

He could also add ½ cup fruit such as blueberries, ½ cup yogurt if desired.

It is best to use the lower fat plain yogurt with the meal.

A Week's Worth of Planning

The logic behind this weekly regimen example involves eating 300 calories on the low-calorie days but can increase to 400 calories if you have an exercise plan in motion.

On the brighter side; women can eat 1200 to 1800 calories on the usual days.

The Low-Calorie Count Days

Day One:

Breakfast

- 1 small slice of deli meat

- 1 six-ounce glass of tomato juice

- ½ cup strawberries

Morning Snack Time
- ¼ cup mixed berries

- 1 tablespoon whey protein

- Blend the ingredients with 3 ice cubes and a cup of water

Lunch
- 1-ounce low-fat cheese

- ½ cup of pickles

- 1-six-ounce cup of tomato juice

Afternoon Snack Time
- 1 tablespoon salad dressing (calorie-free) on one celery stalk

-

Dinner Time
- Make an omelet using three egg whites, mushrooms, green peppers, and onions.

- For dessert have ½ cup of strawberries

Evening Snack
- Whey protein smoothie is your savior to enjoy with a cup of mixed veggies.

Normal Calorie Counted Days

Day 2:

Breakfast
- 1 small banana

- 20 Blueberries

- 1 English muffin (whole wheat) with 2 ¼ teaspoons of peanut butter

- 2/3 cup fat-free yogurt

Morning Snack Time
- 3 saltines

- 1 reduced-fat string cheese stick

Lunch
- 3 tablespoons of hummus with tomato and lettuce

- 1 Whole wheat wrap

- *Dessert*: 1 cup low-fat yogurt and ½ cup of applesauce

Afternoon Snack Time
- 15 almonds

Dinner
- 3 ounces—chicken breast

- 1 cup of broccoli and 2/3 cup of couscous

Evening Snacks
- 1 tablespoon peanut butter on 2 large graham cracker squares

Low-Calorie Day

Day 3:

Breakfast Meal
- ½ fruit serving

- 1-ounce of protein

- 1 six-ounce glass of tomato juice

Mid-morning Snack
- ¼ of a serving of fruit

- *Smoothie:* Combine three pieces of ice + one cup of water with one tablespoon whey protein.

Lunch Menu
- 1-ounce of protein

- 1 six-ounce glass of tomato juice

Mid-afternoon Snack
- Enjoy something under 50 calories.

Dinner Meal
- No more than 100 calories—include protein, veggies, and fruit as a focus point

Normal Calorie Count Day

Day 4:

Breakfast Meal
- 20 blueberries

- ¼ cup banana

- Whole wheat English muffin with 1 tablespoon of peanut butter

Mid-morning Snack
- 2 tablespoons of light cheese

- 3 rye crackers

Lunch
- 6 whole wheat crackers

- 1 cup of vegetable beef soup

- 1 piece fresh fruit

Mid-Afternoon Snack
- 5-6 medium strawberries

- 1-ounce dark chocolate

Dinner Menu
Steak and Peppers

Grill or broil:
1—four-ounce flank steak flavored with pepper and salt

Sauté Pepper Mixture:

- 2 teaspoons red wine
- 1 teaspoon olive oil
- ¼ cup onion sliced
- ¾ cup sliced bell pepper
- 1 tablespoon hoisin sauce

Instructions
1. Over a medium heat setting, sauté each of the ingredients listed using the teaspoon of olive oil.

2. After the flank steak is cooked to your preference, add the sautéed pepper mixture.

Calories: 267 per serving

Method 5:2 and 4:3

For this plan, you would eat a regular diet for five days.

For the remaining two days, you will eat approximately 500 to 600 calories.

The baseline of the calorie ingestion is 2,000 for women and 2,500 for men.

A few famous names swear by the diet including Jennifer Aniston and David Cameron.

These are some of the ways of how to manage the 5:2 diet plan.

Just remember carbs don't mix with your fasting days.

Experiment with Mealtime

- Test different eating times.

  It doesn't always have to be an early time of day when you aren't hungry.

  You can wait a bit longer if you wish.

- Change from eating three meals each day to two such as having brunch.

  It can combine the meals and save the calories.

  Try having brunch around 11 am and dinner at 7 pm, or even a larger meal at 8 pm with your significant other.

Maximize the Flavoring and Minimize the Calories

- Soups are a respectable choice—also proven by research— because you remain full longer than just a modest serving of veggies on a plate.

- Flavor your foods with spices and herbs such as these— lemon juice or vinegar for salads or curry pastes or chili flakes in stews, baked beans, or soups.

- Go for the veggies and salads with smaller servings of fish, eggs, lean meat, or tofu.

Use Fresh Ingredients

- Not only are you eating better and healthier products, but also most fresh ingredients are less expensive.

  Search for seasonal produce for the most savings.

- Search for items such as a tomato that have ripened.

  These will make a yummy treat with a few of your special herbs and balsamic vinegar.

  You could also add it to some soup.

- During the winter months, experiment with butternut squash or parsnip—roasted—with low-fat feta—or in soup.

- Cut some peppers in half and stuff them with cream cheese, tuna, or similar ingredients and grill them.

  You can add an egg to the mix for a taste challenge.

Food for the Fasting Days

- Berries and natural yogurt
- Plentiful veggie portions
- Baked or boiled eggs
- Low-calorie cup soups
- Other soups: vegetable, tomato, miso, cauliflower
- Lean mean or grilled fish
- Tea or black coffee
- Water (sparkling or still)

The 4:3 Diet Plan

Health benefits include asthma relief, reduction in heart arrhythmias, insulin resistance, menopausal hot flashes, seasonal allergies, and much more.

After twelve weeks of fasting using the 4:3 method diet plan, these are the results from a small study group:

- Fat mass reduction: 3.5 kg with no muscle mass changes
- Body weight reduction: Over 5 kg
- Increased LDL particle size
- Reduced blood levels: 20% reduction of triglycerides
- Leptin levels: 40% decreased
- Levels CRP: Reduced levels (inflammation marker in your body)

How the 4:3 Diet Plan is Different from the 5:2 Plan

The 5:2 intermittent fasting choices are much simpler than the 4:3 Plan because you are more restricted.

You will be intermittently fasting for three out of the seven days.

You should not eat processed/sugary/refined foods for four of the days.

If you do, your body will crave the supplementary fatty acids you need to thrive.

If you consume junk on those four days, you will defeat the purpose of the plan.

Just remember, not to over-indulge.

As you train your body by eating a well-planned diet; your body will adjust to the routine, and you won't feel as hungry.

The 4:3 Plan acclaims you skip the morning meal, and it recommends you check your weight daily.

However, this can be disheartening if your weight fluctuates.

A sample plan for the 4:3 method of weight loss is as follows:

- *Breakfast:* Eat nothing.

- *Lunch:* Leek, lentil, or chicken soup with a snack such as a small tangerine

- *Dinner:* A side salad using lemon juice as the dressing with some salt, pepper, or similar seasonings along with a small lean fillet of grilled chicken

- *Snacks:* Veggies or fruit

You can have a light breakfast if you enjoy a morning meal, but you will need to eliminate the snack during the day.

You can also skip lunch, and have a larger breakfast.

This is more challenging to follow than the 5:2 intermittent fasting plan because you have three days you can only consume 500 calories versus two days on the 5:2 diet.

Suggestions for the Fasting Days Using the 4:3 Method

- Drink an abundance of water.

- Drink coffee and tea for an additional boost.

- Consume a 400-calorie meal with a snack of 100 total calories.

- Chew sugar-free gum to fight the hunger spurts.

If you have a busy lifestyle, you can cheat once in a while with a low-calorie pre-packaged meal. (This is not a regular outlet.)

The point in both plans is to eat as much as you want and not feel deprived on the days you can eat normally—just do it in moderation, not over-indulgence.

Chapter 8: Tips and Simple Meal Plans

Simple Guidelines to Follow for Fasting

Stay in Control: Depending on which method you choose for your intermittent fasting routine, you need to ask the question if you can follow the crucial diet plans involved to keep your food intake at proper levels.

If you are attempting to achieve a 500-calorie debit daily, you have to keep your appetite under control, because a single missed meal won't provide a generous window for the next meal.

Keep a Calorie Tally Record: You must keep an accurate record of your calorie intake because if you are not careful, you can easily overeat at mealtime.

If your goal is to work off more calories than you consume to lose the one pound of weight you want to lose each week.

Stay with the Chosen Plan: You need to get into the habit of setting a regular schedule for your fasting plan.

Once your body adjusts to the specific method, it will become confused if you try another plan.

For example, if you are on the 5:2 plan and switch to the 16:8 plan, your body will stop the weight loss until it can readjust to the new plan.

You will lose valuable time by switching.

Consistency is essential for a successful fasting plan.

Breakfasts and Snacks

While you are attempting to lose weight on the intermittent fasting plan, you should not feel the need to be hungry no matter which of the procedures you decide to use.

Some of the recipes call for grams which need to be converted to ounces.

Use this handy chart to calculate the amounts.

This chapter is dedicated to some of the meals you can use.

Each menu plan has a calorie count within the recipe.

Breakfast

Porridge

89 Calories: 25 g Porridge oats
10 Calories: ½ teaspoon honey
0 Calories: Water and Cinnamon

Tips:
Instead of milk, use some water to reduce the calorie count. For some additional flavor add just a pinch of cinnamon. You can also improve the meal with a few nuts if you add the calories to your plan.

Toast and Beans

55 Calories: 1 slice whole- meal bread (small loaf size)
42 Calories: 50 g Baked beans

For a quick and low-calorie choice, tempt your taste buds with this unique idea.

Fruity Breakfast Meals

Watermelon

The natural sugars are more beneficial than a cereal bar.
96 Calories: 300 g serving

Honey and Bananas

10 Calories: ½ teaspoon honey
89 Calories: 1 small banana

Apricots and Yogurt

68 Calories: Two chopped apricots and 25 g Greek yogurt (low-fat)

Apricots, Greek Fat-Free Yogurt, and Mixed Berries

- 24 Calories: 3 tablespoons Greek yogurt
- 17 Calories: 1 Apricot
- 19 Calories: 50 g Raspberries
- 16 Calories: 50 g Strawberries
- 20 Calories: 50 g Blackberries
- Total Calories: 96

Blend the ingredients for a yummy treat.

Greek Yogurt, Sultanas, & Almonds

- 24 Calories: 3 tablespoons Greek Yogurt (fat-free)
- 42 Calories: 1 tablespoon sultanas
- 28 Calories: 4 almonds (whole)
- Total Calorie Intake: 94

Blueberries, Kiwi, & Greek Yogurt

- 42 Calories: 1 kiwi (chopped)
- 29 Calories: Blueberries (50g)
- 24 Calories: 3 tablespoons yogurt

Total Intake: 95 Calories

Mix all the ingredients for a tasty meal.

Raspberry and Cranberry Smoothie

- 14 ounces/175 g raspberries
- 7 ounces cranberry juice
- 3 ounces natural yogurt
- Mint sprigs

For a quick and easy breakfast try this one packing 100 calories per serving.
Serves 4 to 6 people

Eggs for Breakfast

Plain Eggs

100 Calories: 1 large boiled egg
Add a slice of wheat toast with two small poached eggs for a 188-calorie delight.

Scrambled with Mushrooms

78 Calories: 1 medium egg
13 Calories: fresh chopped mushrooms (100 g)
Total Count: 91 Calories

Scramble the ingredients and enjoy!

Spinach Omelet

16 Calories: 60 g fresh spinach
78 Calories: 1 medium egg
Total Calorie Count: 94

Instructions
1. Simply, beat/whisk the egg and place in a frying pay.
2. When the bottom is cooked; add spinach to the top and grill.
3. If you want, you can add some herbs, salt, or pepper for additional flavoring.

Ham Omelet

19 Calories: 1 slice of ham/wafer sliced
78 Calories: 1 Egg (medium)

Prepare the ingredients as above.

Starchy Options

Bread with Honey

55 Calories: 1 slice bread (whole meal from a small loaf)
40 Calories: 2 teaspoons honey
Total: 95

Perfect Pancakes

2 eggs
1 1/3 cups milk (300 ml) 100 g all-purpose flour
Sunflower Oil

Instructions
Blend the ingredients, cook, and sprinkle with a splash of lemon juice.

114 Calories: Per serving
Total Servings: 4

Pancake Variation

2 whole eggs
1 ripe banana

Instructions
1. Simply blend the two ingredients until the bananas are completely mashed.
2. Gently grease a pan with a sprinkle of oil and add the batter.
3. Cook 20 to 30 seconds, flip them over and enjoy.

Calorie counts: 1 medium banana/118 g/105 calories
2 large eggs/100 g/156 calories

A total of 261 calories is not bad for these yummy delights!

In Advance: Fiber-Packed Cereal

If you have a busy lifestyle and always rush in the morning, consider making this tasty breakfast bowl. It will serve 18 meals at 124 calories each.

- 100 g All-bran
- 300 g jumbo oats
- 50 g golden linseed
- 25 g wheat germ
- 140 g ready-to-eat apricots (chunked)
- 100 g dark raisins

Instructions
1. Blend all the ingredients.
2. Ahead of time break down each of the units and store in airtight containers.
3. To serve: Add milk and let it soak. Grate some unpeeled apple over it for a flavor delight.

Note: The cereal can be safely stored for two months in the airtight container.

Snacks

Snack time doesn't always have to be boring.

You can trick your mind by using the small plate.

Add some of these healthier choices to your intermittent fasting meal plan for weight loss.

You will also notice the 'not so healthy' choices are higher calorie content, but that is the advantage of planning your menu before you are hungry.

Each of these yummy delights will keep you going until lunchtime:

- 130 Calories: One square dark chocolate and a small banana
- 55 Calories: 10 g of 85% Dark chocolate
- 75 Calories: 3 Stuffed celery sticks with low-fat cottage cheese
- 96 Calories: 16 olives (green or black)
- 90 Calories: 1 Cup Cherries
- 29 Calories: 100 g Honeydew melon
- 42 Calories: 2 Satsumas/tangerine (The Christmas Orange)
- 90 Calories: 3 thin slices Pineapple
- 61 Calories: 100 g Grapes/ OR 100 Calories: 30 grapes
- 42 Calories: Sun-Maid Mini Box of Raisins
- 90 Calories: 25 Pistachio nuts
- 74 Calories: 10 Salted peanuts

Each Item Counts as 100 Calories:

- 31 Asparagus Spears
- 9—5" Spears of Broccoli
- 16 ribs Celery
- 12 Raw Brussels Sprouts
- 28 Baby Carrots

- 82 Red Kidney Beans
- 60 Raw Green Beans
- 43 Boiled or Steamed Okra Pods
- 100 Radishes
- 20 Sun-Dried Tomatoes
- 22 Cloves Garlic
- 100 Raspberries
- 5 Dried Figs
- 6 Dried Apricots
- 8 Cashew Nuts
- 10 Pringles Chips
- 21 Pretzels Unsalted Minis
- 4 Sardines in Oil Drained
- 13 Large Boiled or Steamed Shrimp
- 15 pieces Dry-Roasted Cashew Halves

Tasty Beverages Too Good to Pass Up!

Starbucks Grande Skinny Iced Latte: 96 Calories

Avocado—Chocolate Milkshake: 169 Total Calories/2 servings

Simply blend and enjoy:

1 ½ cups skim milk
2 tablespoons each:

- Brown sugar
- Cocoa powder

½ ripe avocado
1 teaspoon vanilla extract

These are just a few of the tasty treats you can have in store for you while you are on the intermittent fasting diet plan.

There are many more for you to discover that will have you losing weight and toning those muscles to get fit in no time!

Conclusion

Thank you again for downloading *Intermittent Fasting: Lose Fat, Build Muscle and Get Fit*!

I hope it provided you with the understanding of the wide variety of options you have when it comes to intermittent fasting and how you can best mix and match to find the perfect solution for you.

Making the decision to alter your primary eating patterns is a major one, and it is important that you take the full weight of the decision into account before acting.

If you are convinced that you have what it takes to take full advantage of the benefits that intermittent fasting has to offer, then the next step is to stop reading, and to start fasting.

Choose the type of intermittent fasting that seems like the best fit for you and give it a try.

Try not to become discouraged if you don't receive immediate results.

Make an effort to find the one that's right for you.

Above all, don't rush, and remember, intermittent fasting is a marathon not a sprint, slow and steady will win the race.

Lastly, if you found this book useful in any way, a review on Amazon is always appreciated!

Bodybuilding

How to Build the
Body of a Greek God

Table of Contents

There are no scenarios in which the publisher or the original author of this work can be in any fashion deemed liable for any hardship or damages that may befall them after undertaking information described herein.

Additionally, the information found on the following pages is intended for informational purposes only and should thus be considered, universal. As befitting its nature, the information presented is without assurance regarding its continued validity or interim quality.

Trademarks that mentioned are done without written consent and can in no way be considered an endorsement from the trademark holder.

Introduction

Congratulations on downloading your personal copy of *Bodybuilding: How to Build the Body of a Greek God.* Thank you for doing so.

These days, bodybuilding information is everywhere. Building toned and big bodies seem to be the norm, but is that really what we are looking for?

This book looks at the classic Greek God physique, one that is strong and capable but not overwhelmingly showy.

With big, clunky bodies becoming the norm for good physique these days, we need an alternative for normal people.

The Greek body is one that is built on hard work and military training, not focused on putting in hours of weight training at the gym every day. Instead, Greeks were hard working warriors and farmers and their bodies reflected that functionality.

The following chapters will discuss how to create a modern-day workout with focus on the old Greek ways of bodybuilding in order to build a healthy, strong body that is more than just a showpiece.

Here, we will discuss specific workouts and nutrition plans that will help get your ideal body.

You will discover how important maintaining an overall healthy lifestyle is in creating an ideal Greek body, and how rewarding maintaining your new physique will be to your mental, physical and social quality of life.

There are plenty of books on bodybuilding on the market, but none quite like this. Thanks again for choosing this one! Every effort was made to ensure it is full of as much useful information as possible. Please enjoy!

Chapter 1: Greek Bodies in Art: Drawings and Statues

In order to truly understand what we are striving for with a Greek physique, we must understand the history behind the ideal Greek body, as it is a rich and vibrant one.

First off, the Greek empire existed from 800BC to 146BC, about three thousand years ago. Even though it was so long ago, Greek culture is still influencing civilizations around the world, including in the realm of health and fitness.

A major theme in Greek art throughout the centuries has been good order and form. The goal with any piece of art is to draw the eye and keep it by presenting something that makes sense to the eye and to the brain.

By using subjects that have perfect proportion will keep the eye looking, constantly drawn to the figure. These concepts have reflected into the work of well to do modern artists.

Creating a human form that is ideal and pleasing to the eye to keep people looking was the main focus.

The David, by Michelangelo

The Greek body is considered an ideal standard for a number of reasons, one being the reputation of the Greeks to be a strong and conquering society.

While their capital was in the Greece we know today, its empire reached through the modern day middle east.

Their citizens were considered the most fearsome warriors of the time, and war was glorified.

The strong and pioneering soldiers' body became typecast as the ideal Greek.

What is interesting and often forgotten in modern society is that the Greeks manufactured these ideal images in the likeness of Gods in which they have never actually met.

Just like in all religions, the idea of God is just that, an idea.

We have not seen this figure, but the human mind needs to put an image to the likeness.

The Greeks did just that. Their renderings of Gods and superhuman figures were not out of reality, but out of imagination.

Yes, the figure is generally the same, but lives up to the impossible standards of pure imagination.

These days, our standards are created by Photoshop, an ideal image rendered by the artist that is not a true reflection of reality.

Just like ancient Greeks, we try to live up to these standards unsuccessfully, perhaps because we are not immortal, and cannot dream to be.

We can dream of a perfect form but in nature, that doesn't exist. Sure, nature follows the Golden Rule often, but there are always imperfections.

The Greeks also established the Olympics. They created games in which they could showcase the strength and stamina of their people, something that could not be done with a less than ideal body.

While the focus was on winning sporting events, it also showcased the beauty and power of their ideal bodies.

The first Olympics was held in honor of Zeus, the most respected of their twelve Gods. Interestingly, nudity was common at the games, further showcasing the able bodies of participants.

The belief system of ancient Greece also brought rise to the idealistic body.

In Greek mythology, a total of fourteen Gods exist, all of which have their own strengths.

Zeus was the most powerful, the god of thunder and sky and of others, like Hades, the god of the underworld and Apollo, the god of the sun, among others.

What all of the male Greek gods had in common was their physique.

Regardless of their power and personal strength, their bodies were portrayed in just about the same way, following the natural form of the Golden Rule, a ratio that is most physically appealing to the eye.

Greek art always depicted the Gods as perfect creatures, who existed in a form that is in great proportion.

Some of the most famous artworks and sculptures were created during the classical period of Greece, between about 500 and 300BC.

This period of time has influenced the Roman Empire, and has had the most lasting impression through art and civilization surviving worldwide in modern times.

This is also the period in which Greek artists did their best work to recreate the ideal human form, thought to be a direct liking to the bodies of the Gods.

During this time, the proper ratios of the human body were extensively studied. The Greeks were so obsessed with the ideal human form that they were one of the first civilizations to quantify proper ratios of waist to height, waist and shoulder breadth and much more.

We will discuss these ratios in more detail in the next chapter.

Famous works of art, like Discobolus, a statue of the discus thrower are very iconic in that they show the Greek body in action.

We must remember that the Olympics originated in ancient Greece, and their contenders were the best of the best.

Their bodies were hard and strong, and able to carry out all of the games, including throwing the discus.

This sculpture shows the range of motion, the development of muscle and brute strength required to be an ideal figure.

Another popular Greek sculpture is The David, created by Michelangelo in the Renaissance period.

This sculpture is a work of art that cannot be compared to any other.

It depicts a young man of stellar form simply standing there, at about seventeen feet tall. With a coy smile and unwitting attitude, he simply is in all his glory; a Greek man. The musculature and details of the body show a man in his true, perfect form.

Speaking of Michelangelo, he is also responsible for his works in the Sistine Chapel in Vatican City.

His painting on the ceiling, The Creation of Adam is one of the most famous pieces of art ever created.

This iconic image shows the moment when God first creates Adam, the first human.

It shows the two touching fingers of their outstretched arms.

The bodies of both Adam and God are shown in ideal proportions, typical for Greek art.

We can see the purity of both figures because they have been painted in a way that depicts a flawless body; something to be attained.

Interestingly, the bodies of ancient Greek women and their goddesses are idealized in a much different way than we see in modern times.

Our current standard of beauty says that women should be stick thin yet muscular.

Looking at Greek art, we cannot compare these modern standards to the influences from ancient Greece. In fact, women are idolized as slender yet not stick thin.

They are in proper proportion with their waists more slender than their hips, yet hips were large and showed the ability to bear children, something that was much more important in ancient Greece.

There were no chiseled female chins or emphasis on rock hard abs. It was a much different, more lenient time for women, as their primary role was to be child bearer and caregiver, not like our modern CrossFit warriors.

Similarly, the standard for the male physique has changed as well.

There was a major shift in the late twentieth century that morphed the ideal male figure into that of a superhero.

His muscles must be big and strong, regardless of function. He would often look to topple over as his torso and upper body would be much larger than his lower half.

Think of modern day bodybuilders and men who use steroids to gain mass, yet function isn't always there.

This is so far against the ideal, functional warrior body of the Greek gods.

These days, we have traded function for "gym muscles", those that can bench press three hundred pounds but don't have the functionality to shovel manure in the garden or deadlift boxes in a warehouse.

The Greeks prided their ideal bodies on the ability to fight in wars, maintain their properties and provide food for their families.

They did not have modern day tools and equipment to do the heavy lifting, they did it with brute strength and agility.

Chapter 2: Proportions of Greek Gods

Ancient Greeks took their physiques very seriously.

It was considered a sign of strength, power and virility to maintain a certain physique.

This was modeled after the perfection of Greek Gods, who were immortal and strong.

They even went as far as to consider specific measurements desirable.

Much like bodybuilders today, Greeks were obsessed with obtaining the perfect body.

Overall, the perfect Greek body was one that was functional and strong.

Greece was often in war, and needed healthy, strong fighters to maintain their armies and fight their enemies.

The Greeks were warriors, and it was necessary to have a strong, functional figure to even have a fighting chance against their enemies.

Men trained to be powerful, agile and fast in order to defeat their enemies.

Good fighters were naturally lean, carrying very little fat. They also had strong upper bodies but did not have overly developed arm muscles like current day bodybuilders.

They needed to be able to travel on foot to new fields of battle.

Once they got there, they could not take a break, they needed to fight.

Stamina was a huge part of training. Being able to run long distances then not keel over upon arrival was an absolute must.

Those who could not keep up would be left behind and would be the first to die in the event of battle.

Men trained to survive, not just to look good naked.

These days, there are fewer opportunities to fight in battle, and even our current army has vehicles to move people around and sophisticated weaponry to prevent hand to hand combat.

The Greeks were often face-to-face with their enemies, wielding swords and shields. They needed brute strength to use them and not get tired out easily.

Even men who did not fight in the Greek military were strong.

Those who were not fighting were farmers and workers who spent their day sowing fields and bailing hay.

These men could lift items over their heads while pulling on their livestock. There rarely were situations in which they would need to bench press weights. Instead, they had functional strengths, the kind that gets real work done.

The ideal measurements of a strong working man were as follows: for the bicep, 16.4 inches in diameter.

As compared to modern bodybuilding, this is puny.

The ideal neck is 16.8 inches in diameter, the chest 45.5-inch diameter and forearms should be 13.2 inches in diameter.

This seems like quite a specific ratio to shoot for, and if you were a Greek, reaching these goals was a matter of day to day living.

As for the lower body, Greeks had naturally strong and muscular legs, ones that could run long distances, be agile enough to evade enemies, and strong enough to wrangle livestock and do daily chores.

Again, it is all about function. A perfect thigh is 24.1 inches in diameter and the calf 15.5 inches.

We must not forget that Greeks also had a very strong core.

The abdomen and back are the muscles at the center of every movement. They swing arms and legs in controlled, exact movements. They lift heavy items, including fallen comrades in battle.

These muscles were slender and not overbuilt.

A perfect waist is 31.9 inches, and hips 38.7 inches.

Hearing about these perfect measurements may seem like a turn-off.

How on earth is an everyday person able to meet these perfect standards?

Truthfully, it is a matter of luck when it comes to bone structure that allows your hips to measure 38.7 inches, regardless of fat. Some men are just bigger.

If you feel like this book is no longer for you just based on these measurements alone, don't get discouraged.

Honestly, it will be a miracle to attain and maintain these perfect numbers, so don't focus so much on it.

Instead, we must consider the Golden Ratio, a number that is much simpler to understand.

Rather than focusing on reaching a certain inch, we must look at the overall proportion within your measurements.

A simple equation can get us there: $(A+B)/A = A/B$.

The perfect ratio is 1:1.618.

This is a much more manageable number to work with and can be used to compare all areas of your physique.

The Golden Ratio is actually found everywhere in the natural world, which is why it is so attractive and pleasing to the eye.

The Fibonacci sequence was developed by an Italian Mathematician named Leonardo Pisano in the middle ages.

By definition it is a sequence of numbers that are the sum of the two preceding numbers.

For example, if 1 and 2 are the first two numbers, three, and the sum of one and two would be the third, and five would be the fourth.

In nature, the Fibonacci sequence is all over.

A good example is tree branches.

The top of a tree fans out in a pattern in which the diameter of the tree follows this equation.

Flowers are the same way with their petals, and the seeds in the center of flowers, specifically sunflowers, make a spiral pattern that fits the equation perfectly.

It is only natural then that the human body also follows this natural pattern.

What we see as the perfect human figure is the tapering of the body from shoulders to waist in the Fibonacci sequence.

When it comes to human attraction, men who fit this ratio are considered scientifically more attractive to women.

The human face also follows this ratio. Ideal facial features should be aligned in a way that follows the natural order, and faces that fit this well are considered the most attractive.

Faces of animals are unconsciously judged using the same standards.

There are some more ratios to consider if perfection is what you're after.

Overall, your waist circumference should be 40-50% of your height, with ideal leaning more toward your height.

So, if you are six feet tall, or 72 inches, your ideal waist size is 36 inches.

Knowing your ideal waist size can help you determine your ideal shoulder size as well.

Use the Golden Ratio by multiplying your waist size times 1.618 to get 58 inches.

If your neck size is important as well, ideally it will measure about half of your waist size.

Your chest should also be 1.25 times your waist.

Properly proportion your lower half based on your upper body.

Your calves should measure about the same as your biceps. Remember to measure both at the largest section.

Your thighs should be strong yet slender, about .75 times the circumference of your waist.

To put it into perspective, the ideal body is described as one with broad shoulders, strong but not overly muscular arms.

The chest should be strong, tapering down to a slim, yet muscular core. The legs should be muscular as well, but lean.

This body is meant to work, and muscles are not meant to be shown off.

In clothes, a Greek body looks slender but toned.

There should be no bulging muscles trying to escape your tee shirt.

Wearing tighter clothing will help show off your new physique, but won't be steroid gaudy.

Your muscles should be understated, but the real magic comes out when you hit the beach.

Proper measurement is very important here, especially if you are taking these numbers to heart quite literally.

Measure your waist at the smallest part of your abdomen, just above the belly button.

Your natural waist hints in just a bit, and may not be exactly where your pants fall, although it should be pretty close, unless you like saggy pants.

Make sure to use a proper measurement technique as well. Use a cloth measuring tape that is typically used for sewing.

The flexibility of the tape will give you a more accurate number.

Also, have a friend help you, especially when it comes to measuring arms and legs. Stay relaxed and measure everything as is. You are not measuring the girth of your muscle when flexed, you want the look while relaxed.

Remember that there are certain features about ourselves that we cannot change.

Things dictated by our genetics, like the shape of our faces or the proportions of our bone structures cannot be meddled with (unless you are considering plastic surgery).

What we can do is use good nutrition and targeted workouts to do the best we can to manipulate muscle tone and percent body fat.

Use these measurements as a benchmark in order to guide your workout strategy, not as strict goal number.

Most likely, you will never meet these strict numbers exactly, so striving for it is a waste of time.

Instead, you want to enjoy your great new physique by showing it off, not by measuring yourself and obsessing about the numbers on a daily basis.

Still, in order to determine if your workout and diet program is working, keep track of your numbers monthly.

Keep the measurements as a guideline to make changes to your workouts as necessary.

Chapter 3: How Hollywood Portrays Greek Gods

While lots of things have changed since ancient Greece, our general physique and body make up has not.

It is possible to achieve the same look with some hard work. We have proof this is possible because of the work of many actors who have achieved the Greek body style to portray them in movies.

Remember that the goal is to have a body that is strong yet functionally useful, that's it. Everything else is just for show.

We have seen actors like Brad Pitt transform themselves into godlike forms for movies like Troy, in which he literally depicted a deity on earth, Achilles.

In the movie and in literature, Achilles is a fierce warrior who cannot be defeated.

His strength and agility are unmatched by any other fighter, and he is feared by all. Of course, as the story goes, he is eventually taken down by his only weakness, his heel.

As an arrow strikes his heel in the story, Achilles is killed. In the movie, it takes a few more to the chest to seem more realistic.

If we pick apart Brad Pitt's physique in this movie, we do not see body builder muscles. Instead, his muscles are there, toned, but understated.

His midsection is long and lean with strong, well-chiseled arms and legs. His muscles are not bulging, yet he is able to move quickly, defeating his enemies while swinging his sword and ducking arrows.

While movie magic certainly plays a role in the overall success of his character, proper training and exercise can help the average person look like our friend Brad Pitt.

Remember that in order to be Achilles, it will take some godly intervention and some serious combat training, but we can at least work on the look.

Another great Brad Pitt body movie is Fight Club.

This 1999 gem has Brad Pitt as Tyler Durden, a founding member of an underground fighting ring in which members battle each other with gloves off, no rules action.

Although traditional Greek warfare is out the window here, Brad Pitt carries the same physique as his character in Troy.

He is long, lean and muscular. More importantly, he is quick and smart, able to duck blows and take down his adversaries.

What is different in this movie is how cut he looks compared to Achilles in Troy.

Tyler Durden is meant to look scrappy, squirrely and a little bit crazy.

His face is chiseled, while a bit gaunt. He has very little fat, and his muscles are more defined.

It is implied that his body is there to destroy others, and little else.

While there are many Greek movies out, like Troy, 300 and many of the genre, there are also lots of superhero movies out lately.

We must make the distinction between the typical Greek God body and the Superhero body.

While both are strong and muscular, the superhero body is more of a likeness to the modern bodybuilder.

Bodybuilding took hold in the 1940s, and made the body more of a spectacle than ever before.

Brad Pitt, Fight Club

While chiseled bodies were formerly used for work, the boundaries had been pushed to show just how big muscles could get.

The upper body was usually the biggest, while maintaining a tiny waist. The idea of proper Greek proportions was totally out the window.

Bodybuilding competitions quickly took off, with top contenders having very large, sometimes steroid induced pecs and biceps with tiny, almost womanlike waists.

The addition of orange spray tan and baby oil was simply a bonus.

While a bit exaggerated, the superhero model body took after these images of bodybuilders.

These days, Marvel and other comic book giants have made movies of just about every superhero out there.

Superman and Thor are gracing the covers of DVDs all over the world.

Their upper bodies are large and in charge, almost carrying too much muscle to be any help.

It's a good thing superhuman strength is built into their job description.

Chris Hemsworth plays Thor in the most recent Avengers series and has a typical superhero build.

While his muscle and tone is something to be admired, the look is very different from the Greek ideal, and not what we are going for here.

Cartoon depictions of superheroes are even more exaggerated.

Take a look at the character Metroman in the Dreamworks movie Megamind. His character has a huge upper body and puny waist and legs.

Yes, it's a cartoon but is also a spoof on the modern day overbuilt upper body.

Chapter 4: Get Muscles of a Greek God

Getting the body of a Greek God may actually be easier and more productive than you think.

Remember that ancient Greek ideal bodies were that of functional human beings.

These people worked hard every day, training for battle as warriors or growing crops to feed their families.

They were building muscle by doing physical labor, not putting in reps at the gym. They certainly weren't doing it hiding behind a computer screen.

In order to build a workout routine, we must consider exactly what the Greeks were doing to obtain these bodies naturally and transform that into something we can do at home or at the gym in this modern era.

Several companies exist that purposely (or not) tailor routines that build strength through functional exercise. Perhaps the most popular right now is CrossFit.

Consider what kinds of exercises are done at CrossFit.

It centers around strength training with real life objects like tires.

Kettlebells are good representations of rocks that a Greek would have been hurling out of their garden.

The tires can represent just about anything heavy around their property that needed moving.

Remember that there was no heavy equipment to move large objects, just brute strength and the help of a few neighbors.

CrossFit also combines cardio exercise with weight training, which better mimics a real life work or war situation that a Greek may have been exposed to.

There are hardly any activities that involve only lifting, which is why typical lifting routines at the gym may be doing little for you.

While we will discuss cardio in more detail in the next chapter, just remember that it needs to be integrated into your routine for the best and fastest results.

That being said, a new trend is making it into the fitness world lately.

High intensity interval training, or HIIT for short, combines small bursts of intense cardio activity with weight training.

The result burns fat and builds muscle while saving time.

Many workouts exist online and in fitness centers everywhere.

When it comes to specific weight training, we need to think about what sets of muscles are used the most.

That is actually a trick question, because a well-rounded functional body uses all of the muscles equally.

Traditional bodybuilding has gotten us too focused on hitting the main ones, alternating between arm day and leg day, when in fact, we should be incorporating movements that incorporate all muscle groups in any given workout.

Your body knows how to use all of its strength at once to get the job done, and does not leave the arm muscles to lift something exclusively.

The back and legs help carry the weight. If you were to lift a bag of grass seed above your head while working in the yard, would you exclusively use your arms or would you distribute the weight evenly over your body?

While the Greeks had it figured out, we must find a way to tailor a workout routine to modern times.

Unless you have a physically strenuous job or have resources to work out outside every day of the year, this routine so far does not seem very feasible.

Instead, we need to modify the routine to work in a gym setting, something most of us are familiar with.

The key to the Greek workout routine is moderate weight strength training to build firm and functional muscles.

Making your goal to lift as much weight as humanly possible will get you a superhero style body.

If that's what you are going for, great, but maybe you should be reading another book.

The goal here is to build functional strength without overdoing it.

The good news is, you don't need to spend countless hours at the gym to get a great body, just smart, targeted exercises.

Weight training in the gym no longer means hitting every machine. Think about your current routine and every individual exercise that you do.

As you complete each motion, can you think of a way that you could carry out the same motion in real life?

For example, how often are you, or your Greek counterpart required to deadlift over a hundred pounds?

While a few instances may exist, their bodies are not built to do that on a regular basis because it just isn't necessary.

Same with bicep curls. That is a very specific movement that only targets one muscle. Most likely, they are working their biceps and the rest of their arm muscles at the same time, not individually.

Just looking at the ideal Greek figure, we can tell that they were not bench pressing excessive weight, as their chests were defined but not huge.

While using weight machines and free weights can mimic functional exercise, it can only come so far.

This is why interval training, and doing activities that combine muscle training with real life situations is so important.

There were no gyms in ancient Greece, and nobody was counting reps. That is a modern day institution that does not translate.

Instead, focus your time on taking classes that combine lots of disciplines, and things that the Greeks would likely be doing.

Greek warriors would practice fighting. They wrestled, boxed, and practiced with swords.

Today, we can recreate some of this with kickboxing classes and martial arts training. Of course, the Olympics were founded around the javelin, discus and other common track and field exercises.

Get involved with local teams to practice your long jump and throwing skills. You will be ready to battle the Persians in no time.

The good old calisthenics your grandfather used to do are useful too.

Use body weight exercises like sit ups, pushups and planks to build a strong core.

This variety of body weight exercises combines repetition of movement to increase muscle tone, induce cardio exercise and improve flexibility.

The best part is, these routines can be done just about anywhere and don't require any equipment.

If financial restrictions are keeping you out of the gym, hit the floor and get to some crunches and pushups. Use sturdy tree limbs or buy a pull up bar to practice pull ups.

The idea behind calisthenics is body weight training, and by nature does not require too much equipment or skill.

If working out is new to you and committing to bulky equipment or buying a gym membership isn't for you, calisthenics is.

The best way to go about a calisthenics routine is to pick a variety of exercises to do in a circuit.

Each exercise should focus on a different muscle group and be done to near exhaustion.

For example, choose to do pushups until your arms get a bit shaky, then quickly move on to an abdominal routine.

Do something that works for each muscle group individually until everything has been touched.

In the end, your heart should be pumping hard to get blood to all of your muscles, and you will begin to tone up and slim down.

If you do choose to work outside the gym, either for convenience, monetary reasons or just a change of scenery, channel your inner Greek god.

Poseidon, God of the Sea

Particularly, Poseidon, the God of the sea, did a lot of swimming.

Regular workouts in the pool or local lake will work all of your muscles at once, and the resistance of the water creates just enough pull to really cut and define your body without looking like a gym lunk.

Alternate different types of swimming strokes. Do the breaststroke, which focuses mainly on the chest and backstroke for your back.

Your legs will pretty much be kicking the whole time but alternate between a normal kick and a frog kick to work different muscle groups.

As you get outside, think of the ancient Greek military climbing the Pindus Mountains to reach their enemies.

Those guys were climbing day and night, so a craggy hillside hike will certainly help define those leg muscles while also building cardio stamina.

Gardening, working with animals and construction are other great ways to build your physique.

If you are really dedicated, trade your desk job for a building career. Or, if you like your cushy position, just volunteer with a home building service on weekends.

Starting a garden on your property is much more than planting seeds. It is tilling up the soil, hoeing and clearing weeds and lifting all sorts of tools.

It requires time every couple of days to keep on top of things, so this is a great way to build some accountability into your routine. Plus, the vegetables you grow will make a great addition to your new Greek style diet, which we will talk more about later.

How do you measure your success?

Any bodybuilding website will tell you that signs of progress come with increased tolerance for weight and number of reps.

But we're not going for a superhero, are we?

Your measure for success should come with functional strength.

Find ways to measure your success in real life like a Greek would.

Volunteer to help your friend move heavy furniture. Volunteer with a local construction company and haul some cement blocks.

Regularly test your strength in real life situations.

Following a regular routine of functional strength training should create better ability to lift heavy objects, move them in awkward positions, and give you the stamina to keep going.

To get started, measure your baseline. Do an activity that you know will give you some physical challenge.

Try entering an obstacle course event or just going to a CrossFit class.

Focus on how your muscles feel during and after the exercise.

Are they burning or giving out? This means you have work to do.

On the ancient battlefield, you would already be dead.

Think of your training as a life and death situation, because you never actually know when you may need strength and stamina to save your own life or that of another.

Hopefully, that gives you a little more motivation as well.

After you begin training, do that baseline activity again, and see how you compare.

Hopefully, your muscles will be better able to handle the hell you are putting them through.

Remember that a good workout is always one that challenges you, so don't make your goal finishing with little effort.

This just means that it is time to step it up and rise to a more difficult baseline.

In the course of your new workout regimen, keep the Greek workout philosophy in mind.

There are no workouts, just work.

Greeks exercised and worked their muscles to get things done.

With the invention of computers and heavy equipment to do work in modern times, chances to get this type of exercise are few and far between unless you seek them out.

Tailor your workouts to real life situations, particularly ones that you will encounter in the future.

As you do this, your muscles will lean out and change, with little additional effort and extra reps at the gym.

If you have no idea where to get started, check out Chapter 6 for an 8-week example guide to start your workouts.

Chapter 5: Cutting Fat With Cardio

Those muscles mean nothing if they are hiding behind a layer of fat.

We have talked a lot about muscle tone for an ideal body, but fat plays a major role as well.

You will recall those perfect proportions we discussed earlier in the book.

Adding fat to any area of the body will change your ratios.

Everybody carries weight a little differently, leading to a couple of extra inches here and there.

Nobody ever gains weight evenly across the whole thing.

Some will have a larger belly, larger butt or carry it all in the thighs.

It is insane to ask for zero percent body fat, as fat is actually necessary for life.

It cushions your vital organs and is necessary as part of your skin and brain makeup.

We cannot eliminate it completely, but we can make sure it stays in check and where we want it.

Tone and strengthen all you want, they will not be seen unless you can melt some of the fat that cushions the muscle.

The only surefire way to burn fat in the body is with cardiovascular exercise.

As we have learned from Greek art, the ideal body was toned and taught, not loose and flabby.

If that is your baseline, don't worry, there are lots we can do to fix it.

The current thinking is that the ideal Greek body was about 10% fat, a far cry from the baseline fat level of 25-30% in today's society.

Aerobic exercise, by definition, is anything that uses oxygen to burn energy.

Many types of exercise create this result, but weight lifting is not one of them.

Weight lifting is anaerobic activity, which does not require the use of oxygen to make energy.

To make it simple, exercises that use oxygen are those that make you out of breath, like running or swimming.

Sure, muscles can be built with these exercises as well, but the main purpose for cardio activity is to work the heart muscle and to burn fat.

The heart is literally at the heart of all exercises, pumping blood full of fresh oxygen to cells and muscles in order to keep the movement going.

A strong heart is an absolute necessity to carry out all activities, and it is important that we keep it healthy.

Working out the heart gives us more stamina over time.

Regular exercise strengthens the heart, making it more efficient at pumping oxygen to muscles, which is required for the overall stamina of muscles in the arms and legs.

Working this muscle for an ancient Greek could have been a matter of life and death.

A warrior that was out of shape would quickly lose to an enemy who was in peak performance, simply out of basic health.

If fat is what you're after, aerobic exercise is your key to success.

The body is a complicated machine that runs on several types of fuel.

The body prefers to use energy from carbohydrates as a primary source of fuel.

Carbohydrates are things like pasta, bread and other simple sugars that can be easily be broken down for energy.

As we eat, the body uses a majority of the energy right away, and whatever it doesn't need is stored as fat for future use.

Often times, we eat more than our bodies need at any given time, and lots of food becomes stored as fat.

A few very common misconceptions occur here.

It isn't just excess fat that gets stored as fat. Any excess calories, whether from fat, carbohydrate or protein will be converted and stored as fat, no questions asked.

The body's metabolism is meant to help us survive, and therefore has the ability to keep anything and everything it doesn't need to fit its urgent needs.

It is meant to be kept for times when food is not available.

In this day and age, excess food is a problem not lack of food, for most people.

During the normal course of the day, the body will burn simple sugars it gets from food to perform normal tasks.

A small amount of these sugars are stored in the liver to use for the remainder of the day.

This includes simple walks around the office, getting lunches ready, cleaning the house and so on.

It is only when this supply in the liver runs out that the body must tap into additional resources for energy. This is where aerobic activity really shines.

During high-intensity exercises like running, or even walking long distances, the liver's supply of sugar is quickly depleted, and the body must pull stored energy from fat cells to fuel the body.

During these times, fat is the main source of energy, and will be until the body is replenished with simple sugars from the diet.

It is during these periods that we need to take advantage of the body's natural metabolism to burn fat for us.

The jury is really out on the timing of meals for fat loss.

Based on this theory, one would assume that exercising on an empty stomach would cause the liver stores to deplete much quicker, putting us in a fat burning mode.

However, we know that eating after a workout will quickly stop fat burning and cause us to go back to burning sugar.

While this all seems ideal, we do need to eat at some point, and the liver will have sugars stored no matter what.

What we do know is that exercising on an empty stomach leads to less energy and intensity during the workout, leading to less calorie burn.

Therefore, it is a good idea to fuel up before a workout, but not to overdo it. We will get more into the science of meal timing in the following chapters.

Cardiovascular exercise burns calories more efficiently than weight training, and weight loss in its simplest terms means burning more calories than you consume.

Not to mention that you are still working some muscles while you run or swim, and muscles require more energy to maintain than fat cells, naturally increasing your body's energy needs for the day.

The body continues to burn fat after a cardio workout is over as well, so it is advantageous to wait about half an hour after exercise to eat.

This is said with a word of caution, as people with health conditions like diabetes need to be vigilant of hypoglycemia, where their blood sugar drops dangerously low.

For the typical individual, showering and dressing after a workout is likely long enough to go before having a quick snack.

Beginning an aerobic routine can be a bit daunting, but getting started with simple steps can get even the most dedicated couch potato into shape.

First, you must determine your baseline level.

If just walking to the mailbox makes you feel winded, you will need to take it slow.

If you are reading this book, we would assume your baseline is a bit higher than that. But perhaps you are a dedicated walker and running makes you feel light-headed and nauseous.

Building up cardio stamina is just like weight training. You need to start small and increase your intensity to build upon your success.

Just as you might start with a five-pound weight with your bicep curls, start with just a few minutes at a light jog during your walk.

Increase your heart rate to a safe level, then bring it back down to baseline.

In general, your pace should allow you to sing or carry on a conversation with your partner as you walk or jog.

If you are so winded that you could not do either, your pace is too fast.

It is important to push yourself past your baseline in order to increase your stamina and calorie burning potential, it is the only way to make improvements.

Just like you would push your muscles until they become a bit shaky, you must get yourself a little out of breath to get that heart working and building muscle memory.

Burning fat is not just about intensity. In fact, studies have shown that fat is burned more efficiently at moderate intensity exercise levels.

Working out too fiercely and getting your heart pumping too hard actually works against you.

Remember that the heart's primary job during cardio exercise is delivering oxygen to your muscles for stamina.

If your muscles work too hard and the oxygen cannot get there, the body works in anaerobic mode, burning sugars in the muscle for fuel.

Both aerobic and anaerobic exercises burn energy, but anaerobic exercise produces lactic acid, which makes muscles feel tired and fatigued, increasing the need for recovery time.

Staying within a relatively safe cardio routine will ensure that you build the stamina you need to exercise more efficiently, but will help in recovery time by not exhausting muscles with lactic acid.

Overall, any extra exercise you do will help burn fat and help you reach your goals.

To start a routine, determine your baseline, just as you would with weight training.

Depending on your time schedule, either add a few minutes each day to your cardio workout or increase the intensity.

Adding interval sprints or aiming to walk or jog just a bit faster will slowly increase your stamina and overall ability.

As your heart and lung strength improve, you will likely see this overlap and make daily tasks that were once difficult a whole lot easier.

Being consistent with cardiovascular training is necessary as well.

You can't work out for a week and expect to maintain the same stamina a month later if you don't continue your routine.

The body declines very quickly into couch potato status if it is not regularly worked, so whatever activity you decide to fit into your daily routine, make sure it is manageable, and something you have time to do on a regular basis.

From a health standpoint, exercise is pushed at us from every angle and is a necessary part of good health.

It would be a good idea to rearrange your priorities a bit to put your exercise routine and your overall health at the top of your list.

After all, you can't get everything else you need to do done unless your body is around to do it.

Certainly, we did not mean to skirt past the issue of sugars and calories coming in from the diet.

Surely, a proper diet routine must fit in here somewhere? Indeed it does, so much so that it gets its own chapter.

Learn more about fueling your workouts and reducing fat buildup through diet in Chapter 9.

Chapter 6: Your 8-Week Weight Training Guide

Everybody will have a different starting point, so it is important to tailor this routine to your specific fitness level.

The guide that follows starts with one week of half hour workouts that are meant to progress as weeks go on.

If you feel that starting with shorter workouts is more feasible for your current level, go ahead and cut it in half to start.

The idea is to progress and get stronger based on your baseline, not everyone else's.

Your goal is to get stronger than you are now, not to compete with others.

Also, these exercises are meant to work out all muscle groups.

If former injuries or disabilities make any of these routines dangerous or painful, modify them to preserve your function.

Remember that even Achilles had a weak ankle, so if you do too, don't do exercises that aggravate the problem.

You will notice that there are only workouts scheduled six days a week.

Every good Greek knows that a day of rest and recovery is a key to a healthy body.

Make sure to relax at least one day a week to allow your muscles to fully repair.

Overworking muscles can lead to decreased performance over time, lethargy and even injury.

Who needs that?

All weight training and weight bearing exercises are meant to be done slowly.

The faster you try to complete the exercise, the less energy is used because momentum is used instead of muscle strength.

Take your time and really put in the work.

Never lock elbows or knees, keep the pressure on your muscles to hold up your weight.

Being a true Greek means incorporating more real life exercises as well.

This routine can be used to get a good baseline going, but be sure to incorporate exercises like hiking, swimming, and other more strenuous activities a few times a week for best results.

Week One: Determine your baseline and warm up

This first week should be dedicated to finding out where you stand physically.

Test your overall strength, agility and flexibility with these exercises.

Get started with this set of exercises, which should take about half an hour once you get going.

These exercises are easy to complete and can be done anywhere.

Should you be traveling or in a situation where you have less time or ability to get to the gym, these exercises can be done.

Monday, Wednesday, Friday

- 10-minute jog/treadmill- outside or in place, to increase the heart rate.

- 20 sit ups x 3 sets- may do more if your baseline fitness level is high. Do as many as possible until your muscles begin to tremble.

- 1-minute jog in place to return heart rate to cardio level.

- 20 pushups x 3 sets- do full pushups or on knees per baseline strength. Again, do more if your baseline is higher.

- 20 pull ups x 3 sets- keep back straight, good posture, do not let elbows lock at the bottom.

- 1-minute jumping jacks in place to return heart rate to cardio level.

- 20 squats x 3 sets- no weights required. Weight should be centered on the heel of the foot, stretching down so upper thigh is parallel to the ground.

- 1-minute jog in place to return heart rate to cardio level.

- 30-second plank x 3 sets- keep back straight, complete on elbows or hands. For extra workout, lift feet off the ground a few inches, alternating feet. This will increase muscle strength in the back and butt.

- 1-minute jog in place to return heart rate to cardio level.

- Stretch and cooldown- stretch back, legs, thighs, bend to stretch hamstrings and back.

Tuesday, Thursday, Saturday

- 10-minute jog to get heart rate pumping.

- 20 reps calf raises x3 sets- flex feet lifting heels off the ground, flexes the calf muscle. For added resistance, carry a weight against your chest to mimic increased body weight.

- 1-minute jog in place to return heart rate to cardio level.

- 20 twist squats x3 sets- regular squat, twist to alternating sides to work glutes. Watch form and keep back straight to avoid overly twisting your back.

- Stair climb x3 reps- climb 1 flight of stairs in your home as quickly, yet safely as possible. If you only have one step, hop up and down alternating feet x 20 per rep.

- 30-second side plank x3 reps each side- for more, raise hips down toward the floor and back up instead of staying static.

- 1-minute jumping jacks to return heart rate to cardio level.

- Ab walk-out x10 reps- from standing position, bend and touch your toes. Walk hand out across floor until in a plank position, then back to original position.

- Stretch and cooldown- stretch back, legs, thighs, bend to stretch hamstrings and back.

Weeks 2-3: Double Week One

Very simply, we need to build stamina past our baseline. Take the workout from week one and double everything. The new routine should take about 1 hour. This can be done in two ways:

Variation 1:

10-minute jog, run through calisthenics portion once, followed by another 10-minute jog, then another round of calisthenics.

Variation 2:

20-minute jog followed by double sets of calisthenics.

To switch it up more, change the order in which you do the exercises. Just remember that maintaining cardio in between reps will help burn more fat while you complete your routine.

Weeks 4-5: Add in more targeted exercises

Use your baseline from week one to determine which muscle groups need more attention.

For example, if pull ups and arm workouts were toughest, put your focus there.

Depending on your commitment and availability of time, either add the following exercises into your circuit or trade them out for ones you have mastered.

Remember to keep up cardio in between.

This progression means you may need some extra equipment.

Invest in free weights or get creative around the house.

Empty milk or water gallon jugs filled with water or sand make great weights with handles.

Weights are adjustable by adding or subtracting water.

Keep several sets to mimic weights.

Use a home scale to determine weights or do it by feel.

Arm exercises

- 20 bicep curls x 3 reps: Use free weights or water jugs to create more resistance.

- 20 triceps kickback x3 reps using free weights or other heavy objects.

- 20 triceps extensions x3 reps.

Leg exercises

- 20 Scissor kicks x3 sets- lie on back and crisscross legs back and forth, also great for back and butt.

- 20 Plank leg lifts x3 sets- plank on hands, lift alternating legs as high as possible back and forth.

- 20 Squat sidekicks x3 sets- bend down to squat, when coming up, kick leg out to side as high as possible, alternate legs.

Core exercises

- 30-second wall sit x3 reps- for more, lift legs out one at a time for extra stretch.

- 30 sprinters x3 reps- from back, pull alternating legs to the chest while maintaining crunch position.

- 30 corkscrews x3 reps- from lying position, point legs up in the air, swirling them around the axis for a full stretch. For hip problems, simply raise and lower legs up and down vertically.

Weeks 6-7: Up the Cardio Intensity

Cardio is a big part of this equation.

By now, you should be used to a quick ten-minute interval jog.

Step it up a notch by alternating sprints.

Your ten minutes should include 3 one-minute sprints, running as fast as you can.

Your leg muscles should feel fatigued and shaky, that's how you know you're really working them out.

If you have more time, increase your total cardio time for added fat burning.

Also, increase the incline if possible.

Utilize stairs, incline on the treadmill or naturally occurring hills in your neighborhood.

Good news, this also counts as a great leg workout while getting that heart going.

Week 8: Revisit Baseline

Remember that strenuous exercise you did to determine your baseline?

If you tried and failed at a kickboxing class or CrossFit session, do it again.

Week 8 is all about measuring progress and setting up for another 8 weeks of workouts.

No routine is complete without a bit of tweaking as your baseline changes.

Use this week to redo week 1 and 2 exercises, complete your baseline challenge and prep for the weeks ahead.

If your baseline task is still very challenging, your workouts aren't doing enough for you.

Add more cardio if your heart still races, and add extra weights or reps if your muscles are failing you early on.

If your baseline task is now easy for you, congratulations!

You have reached your goal, and it is time to set a new one.

Try setting something more long term, like entering a strength and stamina competition, a triathlon or other competitive event.

If that's not your speed, try setting up a friendly challenge with people you know.

Getting others involved makes the process of working out fun, entertaining and social, three things that are a requirement for life-long program success.

You surely won't continue working out if you don't enjoy the new lifestyle changes.

Set up a new plan.

After week eight, you are free to use these exercises as you choose.

Create a fun and exciting workout with these movements, add some fresh new things and pair them with cardio exercises that are more stimulating than jogging.

The sky is the limit with exercise, so make it a goal to try some new things to keep it fresh.

Just remember to keep your ancient Greek friends in mind if you do.

Chapter 7: Proper Nutrition

Working out means nothing if you are not properly fueling your body.

Everywhere you look there is advice about proper eating techniques for your best body, and this book, too, will provide its own advice.

The difference here is that we will look at nutrition through the eyes of those we look to become, the ancient Greeks.

First, let's take a look at the science behind food.

It is important to know how different types of foods interact with our metabolism.

There are three major components of food; protein, carbohydrates and fat.

Each can be used for fuel in the body, as our metabolism is equipped to utilize anything available for survival.

As we discussed in the chapter on cardio exercise, simple sugars broken down from carbohydrates are the body's primary source of fuel.

The simple sugars that make up carbohydrates are not bound to other compounds and can chemically be broken down very quickly.

If the body was starved for fuel, carbohydrates can be utilized before the body expires.

In fact, carbohydrates serve no other purpose in the body except for energy.

These little nuggets of energy can be stored within the liver short term, or packed away and stored as fat for later use.

Because carbohydrates are so readily stored as fat, they should be limited in the diet.

Heavy carbs like potatoes and pasta should be limited or eliminated, while lower carb fruits should be chosen in their place.

Fruits also provide fiber, which cannot be broken down and used for energy, but helps keep the digestive tract moving.

Increased fiber keeps you full longer as it takes so much time to be broken down.

Protein from the diet is what muscle is made of, and will be the key ingredient to keeping muscles healthy and toned through your exercise regimen.

As muscles are worked, the fibers that make them fray and break, and must be repaired.

Protein from the diet is quickly shunted to muscles in need of repair to rebuild them quickly.

Proteins from the body are broken down into amino acids, which help build and repair muscles.

Protein can come from both plant and animal sources, however, animal proteins like chicken and fish provide a more complete amino acid profiles necessary for repair.

If you think about it, you are eating muscle from another animal to supplement and repair your own muscle.

Using plant proteins like soy will not give you the same variety of amino acids your muscles need to rebuild.

Dietary fat has a really bad reputation, one that is totally unwarranted.

Fat is a necessary nutrient to life and is absolutely essential to the function in our bodies.

It is responsible for cushioning our vital organs, works in cells to facilitate chemical reactions that drive life, and actually make up the majority of our brain mass.

We literally cannot think straight without fat.

Fats aid in the digestion of fat-soluble vitamins, help with hormone reactions, and a number of other supportive roles.

Yet, modern day diets have shunned fat, calling it the responsible party for weight gain.

Per gram, provides the most energy of the three macronutrients, and this is why the mob is after it.

A little bit of fat goes a long way, with just a teaspoon of olive oil carrying about one hundred calories.

In the past, it was thought that dietary fat was solely responsible for increasing fat stores in the body.

We now know that is untrue, as excess carbohydrates are more a culprit for fat storage than dietary fats.

Not all fats are created equal, and it is still necessary to use them sparingly because of their high-calorie content.

Small amounts of polyunsaturated fats, like olive oil and avocado keep the body running like a well-oiled machine.

Saturated animal fats like lard and butter should be eaten sparingly if at all, as they are transported through the blood in cholesterol.

Excess saturated fat increases cholesterol and blocks arteries causing heart disease.

Let's put this all together.

We now know that we need a variety of carbohydrates, protein and fats for a healthy body, despite what fad diets sling out for information.

The key is that we get them all in a balanced way.

In general, our plates should be balanced at every meal.

Focus half of your plate around non-starchy vegetables like salad, cooked broccoli, asparagus or tomato.

Potatoes and corn are considered starchy vegetables and should be considered a carbohydrate.

The other half of your plate should be split evenly between lean protein and carbohydrate.

Fats should be used sparingly, and consider them as a garnish.

If you like oil or have cooked the meat or vegetables in oil, stick to 1-2 teaspoonfuls per meal maximum, and make sure they are good quality oils like coconut, olive or avocado.

A common thread with bodybuilding is the use of excess protein to build muscles.

There are shelves full of products in health food stores that are loaded with amino acids for building muscles.

But what are the real benefits of that?

If you are a professional body builder in the business of growing massive muscles, extra protein will be required.

As we discussed earlier, breaking down muscles with exercise requires protein to build them back up.

Theoretically, if more protein is available, the muscle will prefer to bulk up with more fibers to be able to handle the extra weight next time.

This is simply physiology and is how to create stronger muscles.

Remember though, that our goal here isn't to create extreme muscles, it is to build upon the ones we have to make them more functional.

This doesn't require too much protein.

In fact, giving more protein than the muscles need will cause the excess to be converted and stored as fat.

Unless you are truly wearing out your muscles, excess protein means excess fat, and isn't that just a waste?

Instead, focus on getting the right amount of protein.

For the majority of healthy people, this equals out to 0.8grams of protein per kilogram body weight.

If you have some weight to lose, your protein needs will actually be a bit higher while you ration your portions down.

In general, if you are at your approximate goal weight, within ten to twenty pounds, use your actual body weight to determine your protein needs.

For example, a 180-pound man, 82 kilograms, will need about 66 grams of protein daily.

Exceeding this will only cause you to overstep your calorie needs for the day, leading to weight and fat gain.

If you are not sure how many calories you will need to maintain or lose weight, consult with your health care professional.

In general, it takes a deficit of 250 calories per day through diet and exercise to lose one pound per week, which is generally regarded as safe weight loss.

To determine what an appropriate weight is for your height, meet with your doctor or registered dietitian to set appropriate goals and get help with meal planning.

All of this is good advice, but how would the Greeks react to this meal pattern?

Honestly, it would probably follow their diets pretty closely.

The last century has brought so many bad things into our diets.

Advancements in food science allow foods to be preserved longer, but the preservatives are unnatural and make us sick.

Using things like high fructose corn syrup to make things taste sweeter has made once very enjoyable treats like fruit bitter and unappealing, leading the way for sugary drinks and snacks to make up the majority of our diets.

The typical American diet now consists of mostly carbohydrates, fat and salt, as this is what we have determined tastes good.

Unfortunately, these foods are high calorie and everything that our bodies do not need right away is stored as fat.

Not to mention the excess salt has our blood pressures through the roof.

Combine the overfeeding with under exercising and we have a recipe for obesity and disease, far from the Greek ideal we are setting out for.

Given that the world we live in is not conducive to a healthy lifestyle, we must look back to determine what worked well for our ancient Greek friends.

In that region during that time, there were only a few major food groups available.

First, there certainly were no processed foods, so they were automatically healthier.

The Greeks ate whatever they could forage or farm.

They had livestock which gave them milk and cheese.

They grew olives, a great healthy source of fat.

In summer months, they had an abundance of fresh fruits and vegetables, and for those who lived by the coast, endless supplies of seafood rich in healthy Omega 3 fatty acids.

They also cultivated grains, giving them bread and other cereal-based treats.

Most importantly, food was work.

These people did not just head to the grocery store to pick these things up.

They worked away on homestead farms, tending to livestock and crops on a daily basis.

An ounce of food was worth a day of work in those days, and everything was eaten in moderation to make it last.

Also, the Greeks did drink a bit of wine, so feel free to have some.

A glass a day has been proven to improve memory and cardiovascular health, just don't overdo it.

Take a note from ancient Greece and model your diet around what was available to them.

This will automatically eliminate a number of things that are contributing to the decline of health.

Eat whole, unprocessed foods from quality sources. Pick fresh fruits and vegetables, and high-quality lean meats.

Given this modern age, indulge in a few decadent treats here and there but if your goal is to look like a Greek warrior, you must act like them.

Chapter 8: Health Benefits of This Program

The goal of this diet is not just to have a great body, but to be healthier.

By following this diet and exercise advice, and striving to have a naturally lean and powerful body, you will be healthier than the majority of people out there.

Here, we are not striving to be bodybuilders, but to have bodies that can build things. There is a major difference.

People who use steroids and overwork their muscles for sheer size will not win out in the end.

Using artificial means to gain muscles that are good for nothing will not lead to good health.

Professional bodybuilders often leave good health in the dust for size, but do not often work on their cardiovascular health, or worry about how their kidneys are handling the supplements they take.

On the flip side, the idea of creating an ideal Greek body is all about good health the natural way.

Using proper diet and exercise techniques nurtures the body without creating extra stress.

Remember that bodybuilders often stress and tear their muscles, leaving their body in a constant state of repair.

While a bit of this is necessary, the body actually hates it.

Your immune system becomes heightened when it thinks it is under attack, and constant muscle repair indicates that you are fending for your life on the outside.

For your body's sake, pair moderate exercise with regular rest to make sure your body is comfortable and stress-free.

If your immune system is taxed, it means it is not taking care of infections and disease that is floating around your body like it should.

While that body builder seems healthy now, their health will likely take a turn if they continue burning both ends of the candle.

In order to reap the health benefits of ancient Greeks, you must truly embrace the lifestyle.

Greek gods and warriors lived in a much different time.

They lived in an era before modern conveniences and were a much busier people.

There was no time to sit around, and really no reason to as television, video games and computers had yet to be invented.

Instead, these people were active in their communities, out enjoying nature, and for a select few, training to become Greek warriors.

Should you embrace the Greek lifestyle and live with the purpose of creating a body that is both healthy and functional, you will reap the benefits, and they should be obvious.

First, you will likely get the body you always dreamed of, which is probably what attracted you to this book.

Working out and fueling your body only with what it needs will lead to great muscle tone and decreased fat.

You will look great at the beach and your friends will wonder how you did it.

The health benefits of a trimmer body are also a great reason to get started.

Having a body that is within a normal weight for your height will decrease your risk of all sorts of health problems.

Obesity is associated with heart disease, diabetes, cancer and a host of other problems as weight increases.

Being in better health overall slows the aging process by creating less stress on your entire body, especially your heart and joints.

Eating better, a major component of this program will also ensure that your body stays in tip top shape.

Limiting bad fats that lead to plaque buildup and heart attacks is a major benefit of this plan.

Also, avoiding processed foods means avoiding chemical fillers that tax the liver and kidneys, and have the potential to cause cancer.

Regular exercise, especially those targeted toward increasing functional strength and cardiovascular stamina mean a healthier heart and lung system as you age.

Starting off strong now means less likelihood of steep decline, and starting from a better point of function improves your overall survival into older age.

Good nutrition and exercise also boost your immune system, giving you the ability to fight off infection.

Besides the physical health benefits, we must also look at mental health.

Studies in recent decades have shown that regular exercise and a great diet keep your brain healthy and decrease the chances of having mental health issues like anxiety, depression or other mood disorders.

The combination of healthy fats and flow of oxygen, among other things, keeps the brain fresh and active.

Being in better health overall can help you socially and financially as well.

Being in better shape means you will likely feel more confident about yourself, leading to more social interaction.

Those who have better social skills say they have a better overall quality of life and a better support system.

Being more social may also mean making the connections necessary to further your career.

Networking is key to being successful at any job.

Yes, you may be good at your job, but do you have the confidence to show it off?

If not, it is time to get your physical and mental health in order to make sure you get noticed.

Make a positive step in your life by committing just eight weeks to trying the Greek lifestyle.

Use the exercise regimen and diet advice to transform yourself physically and mentally.

Getting healthier, despite specific Golden Rule measurements will improve your life dramatically.

Reap the health benefits by making this advice part of your overall lifestyle.

Live a better quality of life by being more active and present in your daily activities.

Conclusion

Thanks for making it through to the end of *Bodybuilding: How to Build the Body of a Greek God*.

This text has been about much more than creating the body of a Greek god.

We must remember that to be a god we must exude confidence and power.

Yes, this begins with confidence in a physical capacity, but also transcends into many other aspects of our lives.

We cannot overlook the overall lifestyle that Greek warriors led in order to achieve these ideal bodies.

They were active members of society, and used brute strength and stamina on a daily basis, chiseling their bodies without even trying.

This was followed up with a healthy diet of foods they grew and raised themselves, putting in energy that is not necessary with our modern conveniences today.

Let's hope it was informative and able to provide you with all of the tools you need to achieve your goals of living like a Greek god.

If you hope to have the body of a Greek god, you must learn to adjust your lifestyle to one which supports the maintenance of this body.

Surely, the exercise program outlined in this book will set you well on your way, but eating like a modern American and sitting for the majority of the day will not give you lasting results.

Make some positive changes that will make it easy and sustainable to have a great body, rather than forcing it into an otherwise lethargic and gluttonous lifestyle.

The Greeks were truly healthier beings, and that should be the point to strive for. A rocking body is just a bonus.

Finally, if you found this book useful in any way, a review on Amazon is always appreciated!

Strength Training (Secrets):

The Best Tips and Strategies to Getting Stronger

Table of Contents

There are no scenarios in which the publisher or the original author of this work can be in any fashion deemed liable for any hardship or damages that may befall them after undertaking information described herein.

Additionally, the information in the following pages is intended only for informational purposes and should thus be thought of as universal.

As befitting its nature, it is presented without assurance regarding its prolonged validity or interim quality.

Trademarks that are mentioned are done without written consent and can in no way be considered an endorsement from the trademark holder.

Introduction

Congratulations on downloading Strength Training Secrets: The Best Tips and Strategies to Getting Stronger and thank you for doing so.

The following chapters will discuss how eating healthy and ensuring you receive plenty of rest is not only beneficial to your body normally, but also how it affects your strength training regimen.

We will go over the basics of strength training and how to get started if you have never done anything like it before.

This will then lead us into the 5x5 workout and some of the best workouts for your legs, chest, and back.

We will also discuss the royalty of strength training: the Squats.

After that I will show you some recipes that are ideal for all your nutritional needs so that you can come up with a meal plan during your exercise program.

There will also be a glossary for some of the terms you may not know so that you are able to easily reference those words as you work your way throughout this book.

Every aspect will be covered for each workout.

I will tell you how to not only perform each workout, but also ensure you know the proper form for each.

There will also be pictures for each workout so that you are able to visually see how each workout should be properly done.

There are plenty of books on this subject on the market, so I wish to thank you again for choosing Strength Training Secrets: The Best Tips and Strategies to Getting Stronger!

Every effort was made to ensure it is full of as much useful information as possible. Please enjoy!

Chapter 1: Healthy Eating & Rest

Healthy Eating

10 Foods for Building Muscle Mass

1. Healthy Fats	6. Cottage Cheese
2. Fruits & Vegetables	7. Eggs
3. Whole Grains	8. Skinless Chicken
4. Oatmeal	9. Whey Protein
5. Tuna & Other Fish	10. Lean Beef

Making sure you eat healthily can be difficult if you are the type of person who has never watched what they ate but it will play a crucial role during your strength training regimen.

It affects everything in your day to day quality of life, from energy, to having healthy skin, to also maintaining a healthy digestive tract.

It is recommended to eat every 3 hours to keep your metabolism up and to also ensure you are having an adequate intake of calories.

It is especially important to have enough calories throughout the day since you will be burning a lot during your workouts.

The goal is to gain muscle, not just to lose weight.

That will come with the workouts as you replace unwanted fat with muscle.

You will also feel less hungry throughout the day.

By replacing larger meals with smaller ones more periodically throughout the day, your stomach will shrink in size.

You will also have fewer cravings because your body will not become so hungry that you feel the need to stop at the closest vending machine to load up on junk food.

If you eat on a routine basis your body will become used to eating at those times.

So say you generally wake up at 6 am, you would then make a routine to eat at 8 am, 12 pm, 5 pm and maybe again at 8 pm.

The first step to eating healthy is to begin with eating a nice healthy breakfast.
When you do so, you will gain energy for the first hour and you will be less hungry throughout the day.

One example of a good breakfast is to have an omelet.

They can be packed with not only protein from the eggs, but you can add lean beef in it as well for a boost in protein.

You can also add veggies which will make your meal have an added nutrition boost.

Also, make a smoothie or shake to have with your meal.

This can be packed with fruit and veggies, oatmeal, and/ or your whey protein.

For a side, you can also add some cottage cheese.

The next step is to make sure you are eating protein with every meal.

Your body needs protein to build and sustain the muscles throughout your body.

Furthermore, it helps with losing fat because it has a high thermic effect on the body.

Now you are probably wondering how much protein intake you should have a day.

The rule of thumb is that for every pound you weigh needs to be converted to 1 gram of protein taken in.

Therefore, if you weigh 180 pounds, you should have a protein intake of 180 grams.

Eating whole protein is the easiest way to help make sure you are getting adequate amounts.

This includes pork, beef, chicken, tuna, salmon, eggs, dairy, and whey (although this is not necessary, it is good to have a whey protein shake after your workouts).

The next thing you want to make sure of is that you are eating fruits and vegetables with every meal you eat.

Most fruits and vegetables are low in calories and you can eat them until you have a full stomach.

They are also jam packed with things that are good for you such as antioxidants, vitamins and minerals, and even fiber which aids your body in digestion.

Without the proper amount of digestive enzymes, your body will actually break down tissues. This includes muscle tissue.

This is why it is crucial for bodybuilders and anyone else who is looking to gain muscle mass include plenty of foods in their diet that contain digestive enzymes.

This means staying away from processed foods, as they do not have any and also not having their meat too well done, as the process of cooking the meat cooks away the digestive enzymes from the food.

If people who are trying to gain muscle pay enough attention to their intake of these digestive enzymes, they will see far better results than someone who does not.

You should only eat carbs post workout. Many people eat more than they should which is why it is recommended to only eat them after working out.

Again, eat fruits and veggies with all of your meals. There are exceptions to this rule though, which are carrots, raisins, and corn.

Eat carbs only after you are done working out (unless you are skinny and wish to gain weight).

Instead of eating white carbs (which you want to avoid) try whole grain foods instead.

If you ARE the thinner individual who would like to gain weight, you can eat carbs after you are finished working out and again after that.

You can eat more as well if it is needed.

You should only consume healthy fats. They increase fat loss and improve overall health.

They also satisfy hunger, are cheap, and they digest slowly, meaning you will stay full longer.

Make sure you avoid artificial trans- fats and margarine.

You will want to make sure your fat intake is well balanced.

Saturated fats such as red meat, increase testosterone levels.

Monounsaturated fats such as mixed nuts protect against cancers and heart disease.

Polyunsaturated fats such as those found in fish oil not only increase testosterone but they also decrease inflammation and promote fat loss.

Make sure you drink plenty of water. The rule of thumb is to consume 1 gallon of water per day. It not only prevents dehydration due to the loss of water through sweating during your workout, but it also staves off hunger.

You will feel hungry if your stomach is empty. This can be done easily by drinking 1 cup of water as soon as you wake up.

You will also want to make sure you are drinking 2 cups of water with every meal and also drink it while you work out.

You will want to ensure that 90 percent of your food intake is whole foods. This means that they are unprocessed and unrefined. Some examples of this are: fish, poultry, fresh meat, fruits, veggies, legumes, etc.

Processed foods such as bagels, fruit bars, pizza and even supplements contain extra sugars, sodium, and a lot of other chemicals.

Here is an example of what your daily diet would consist of:

- Breakfast- omelet with veggies, an orange, and some green tea
- Snack- a pear and some mixed nuts
- Lunch- some romaine lettuce, tuna, olives, and olive oil
- Snack- an apple and a serving of cottage cheese
- Post workout- a banana, some spinach, quinoa, and some lean beef
- Dinner- baby carrots, chicken, spinach, and a pear
- Before bed- fish oil, ground flax seeds, a serving of cottage cheese, and berries

Many people nowadays are vegetarian.

So you may be wondering how a vegetarian can possibly get enough protein intake and hold onto their beliefs.

Protein can also be found in beans, nuts, legumes, seeds, milk (soy, almond, etc.), veggies, whole grains, and protein powder.

Here is an example of what a vegetarian diet would consist of:

- Breakfast- an orange, whole eggs and spinach
- Snack- an apple and some mixed nuts/ seeds
- Lunch- legumes and soy burger
- Snack- a smoothie that has fruit and veggies with whey protein powder
- Post workout- 1-liter soy or almond milk with a banana or strawberries (or both)
- Dinner- tofu and some mixed beans
- Before bed- ground flax seeds, some berries and a serving of cottage cheese

Rest

You are pumped about gaining muscle as soon as possible. You want to plan on going to the gym every day. DON'T.

Anyone can tell you this is a bad idea. Why? Because working out every day does not allow your body the adequate amount of time it needs to be at peak performance.

Simply said, you will not see the gain you are hoping to if you do this. Your muscle gain will suffer more in the long run.

What if I work on different parts of my body each day? It does not matter. Your body as a whole needs to rest.

When you work out, you are putting stress on your body. That stress that your body is feeling takes more than 24 hours to recuperate.

It is recommended that you give your muscles 48 hours to rest. This means that you pick a day you want to work out, you can do your legs and chest that day. The next day, refrain from going to the gym. Instead, focus on your mobility. Spend this day doing various stretches.

Eating healthy also affects your recovery time, which for a muscle to fully recover, takes approximately 7 to 14 days.

If your body has the proper vitamin and other nutrients it needs, it will have the fuel it needs to recover quickly.

One way to help this is by having a whey protein shake after you are done with your workout. This helps your body to rebuild muscle tissue lost during your workout.

Rest isn't all about the rest period between sets or workouts though. It's also about the amount of sleep you get every night. The longer you sleep and the better quality of sleep you have each night also affects your recovery time.

Generally, people who work out regularly sleep longer and have a better quality of sleep.

Someone who is physically active requires more sleep at night than if they were just going about with normal, everyday activities.

The more physically active you are, the more sleep you need. This is because there is more stress on the muscles and nervous system. The rebuilding that is required for the most part is done while you sleep.

So the more you do, the more rebuilding is required for that system. If you do not get an adequate amount of sleep, you open yourself up to the possibility of getting infections. This, in turn, leads to compromised training.

One side of overtraining is the inability to sleep or remain asleep. If this happens while you are working out, tone it down a little. Instead of lifting 100 pounds, try lifting 80 or 90 pounds.

You should not train too early or too late in the day. If you attempt to train early after waking up, you will still be groggy throughout your workout. This means you will not be able to give the workouts the 100 percent focus that they should receive.

If you attempt to perform your workout too late in the day, it will be similar. You will be too worn out from the day to fully focus on your training. Also, in order to get proper sleep, your body will need to already be somewhat relaxed when you go to bed.

If you are tired or stressed from a good, hard workout, your sleep will suffer.

There is a higher level of arousal with heavy workouts.

The bottom line is that your workouts need your full commitment. This is why many people who lift prefer to do their workouts in the afternoon.

At the end of the day, your commitment and recovery need to be your top priority if you want to be involved in intense training.

If for any reason you are unable to get the proper amount of sleep at night, do not hesitate to take a nap during the day. You can take a short nap before your training, after, or both.

Napping can be useful to get some recovery time in in the middle of the day. This can also make your day go by smoother and easier.

During REM sleep, the growth hormone that is commonly received through supplements is released. This helps the body to repair old and/ or malfunctioning cells.

While you are awake, stress hormones are released and to some extent suppresses your immune system.

In order to have good sleep hygiene, you will need to limit how intense your evening activities are and begin to practice an evening ritual.

It is ideal that two hours before bed, you cease any activities that cause you stress.

Calming ritual behaviors such as brushing your teeth, taking a shower, and/ or reading a book are the ideal.

Another way to help your sleep hygiene is to create the perfect sleep environment.

Buy curtains that completely block out sunlight. Make it silent by closing the windows and regulate the temperature by adjusting the thermostat. Also, try to avoid drinking any caffeinated beverages such as soda and coffee in the evening.

Alcohol is okay as long as it is consumed in moderation.

Chapter 2: Beginner's Guide

Types of Training

Bodyweight: There is little to no equipment needed. You can exercise anywhere that provides enough room to move around.

Exercise bands can help you with movements like pull-ups or dips. Continuously modify the exercise to make sure that you are adding difficulty each time and therefore increasing your progression.

Dumbbells: Most gyms have them. If you wish to train at home, there are adjustable dumbbells that require very little room.

They add some weight to movements and are less overwhelming than barbell training. They can help to identify any muscle imbalances easily.

You can also drop a dumbbell easier than a barbell. The disadvantage to this type of training is that you can outgrow the set you purchase quickly but this can be counteracted by obtaining a gym membership with a set up to or over 100 pounds.

Barbells: Perfect for people who want strength more than anything. You can progress quickly and add a small amount of weight each week.

This is more stable because you must use two hands and is easier to go heavy, particularly for lower body movements like squats or deadlifts.

The disadvantage of this type of training is you would need a bench, squat rack, barbell, and enough weights in your garage or house.

How do I know which one is right for me?

Pick the one you know you can and WILL do.

Bodyweight training is convenient but requires motivation. If you are not self-motivated, this will probably not be the option for you.

One way to overcome this is to set your alarm a little earlier in the morning and make the conscious choice that no matter how you are feeling, you will get up, get your exercise in, and eat a proper breakfast. After a while, you will not have to even think about it and you will notice that if you skip a day, you will not feel as great as the days when you are working out.

Barbell training is best for strength training but requires traveling to the gym three times a week. If you foresee this being an issue, choose something else more realistic for you.

Remember that no matter which type you choose to be your main, a well-balanced, functional body is made by blending all three types of training.

Other fun ways to do strength training is rock climbing, yoga, and parkour.

You should look for a proper workout program for beginners. Ensure the difficulty increases over time.

You want to always do better than the previous day by doing another squat or lifting a few more pounds. This ensures you are continuing becoming both stronger and faster.

Make sure you always start with your body weight and something like a broom handle or something similar to simulate a barbell until you have the form down. This will protect you from injury.

Also, make sure you have water available and a notebook to track your workouts and improvement. Bring clothes to exercise in if you are planning on going to the gym after work.

I've heard of overtraining. What is it and how can I avoid it?

Overtraining is to train or cause to train too hard or for too long. Sometimes it is done due to the person not being happy with their results from a short period of exercising/ lifting.

4 Factors that separate those who struggle with overtraining:

1. Under- recovering: If you do not supply your body with its needs or not training within your activity threshold then you may develop the following symptoms: anxiety, stress, slowed metabolism, lowered mood, suppressed appetite, hormonal imbalances, missed menstrual cycle, sleep disturbances, and fatigue.

You can prevent this from happening by: sleeping 7-9 hours per night, eating plenty of real food, not relying on caffeine or sugar, digesting food properly, drinking plenty of water, varying the intensity of your workouts, stretching and working on mobility, and other recovery hacks such as massage and chiropractic therapy, ice baths, infrared saunas, etc.

2. Work Capacity: When you go over your threshold too quickly or too often, you hurt yourself more than you help it. Train according to your body type.

3. Mindset: Simply you need to develop the positive mindset to succeed in the gym.

4. Underlying Imbalances: Your current state of health plays a crucial role in your ability to slowly correct any imbalances the body may have.

Reps change the outcome of the exercise

- 1-5 build dense muscle and strength

- 6-12 build equal amounts of muscle strength and endurance

- 12+ build muscular endurance and size

Beginner Bodyweight Workout

- 5-10 minute Warm Up
- 20 Body Squats

- o 10 Push Ups (If you are unable to do the normal ones, try doing a modified version such as Wall Pushups until you can more upper body strength.)
- o 20 Walking Lunges
- o 10 Dumbbell Rows (use a gallon of milk)
- o 15 second Plank
- o 30 Jumping Jacks

-Repeat 3 times-

If you want to just have a day solely consisting of squats:

5-10 minute Warm Up
10 Squats
2-3 minute Rest period
10 Squats
2-3 minute Rest period
10 Squats
2-3 minute Rest period

Chapter 3: 5x5 Workout

Popularized by Bill Starr in his book, written in 1976, called "The Strongest Shall Survive: Strength Training for Football", the 5x5 workout has been used by top bodybuilders such as Arnold Schwarzenegger.

It was designed and intended to have the trainee work out hard for 3 days out of the week. It then provided the muscles with the rest of the days to recover and stimulate growth.

You will see an increase in muscle mass as long as you are eating an adequate amount of calories. The volume and intensity are both higher compared to other routines. Your body will have a hard time recovering if it is not used to the higher loads.

This workout is 7-9 weeks (4-6 weeks of prep work, 3 weeks peak phase, 1-week deloading).

Prep work consists of picking a weight you can do 5 sets of 5 reps of. It should not be easy.

You don't want to feel like you can do more but also not so hard that you cannot complete the workout.

Prior to beginning you will want to set a max of 5 reps for each exercise so you know the weight you'd like to beat.

You will need to figure out how much you can lift doing the 5 sets of 5 reps.

Take the highest weight and divide it in half. It may not seem like much, but you will need to remember that you will be adding 5 pounds each time you do the exercises, and adding 10 pounds each time you do the deadlift.

Only do this though if you are able to reach all 5 sets of 5 reps.

When you go 3 consecutive workouts without being able to do all 5 sets of 5 reps, you will need to into the deload section of your program.

This is when you subtract 10 pounds from your next workout. This is only meant for one training session. After that, you will try again. Track your progress to help you keep track of your gains.

One of the most popular 5x5 workout programs is from StrongLifts. But how do you know if it is right for you?

You can choose to take a random approach to it and do random exercises for as long and hard as you can. Or you can follow a program that was carefully and meticulously planned to give you the best results possible.

These exercises are manipulated over time for better intensity and volume.

Making sure you pick the right program is crucial for better progress, fewer injuries, and making sure you push yourself as hard as you possibly can both night and day.

So how does StrongLifts 5x5 program work?

For this program, you only work out three days a week using two workouts.

Workout 1: Bench Press 5×5, Squat 5×5, Barbell Row 5×5

Workout 2: Overhead Press 5×5, Squat 5×5, Deadlift 1×5

For each lift, you perform 5 sets of 5 reps, with the exception of the deadlift, which is 1 set of 5 reps.

Although it seems strange, according to StrongLifts, doing any more than that would cause undue stress on your body and the squats will work many of the same muscles as the deadlifts.

This is not a bodybuilding program. The point of it is to train in a somewhat small rep range in order to increase strength.

Your goal will be to increase the amount that you are lifting by 5 pounds each time you do each workout for as long as you can until you peak.

These are separate and will not vary in weight.

A two-week training cycle would consist of working out every Monday, Wednesday, and Friday, resting in between each and alternating workouts each time.

There are several advantages to doing the 5x5 workout program. This is especially true for beginners. They generally tend to attempt complex routines which does more harm than good because they do not yet have the base knowledge that they need in order to do them.

The 5x5 workout program is simplicity at its finest. You know how many days out of the week you need to train and what exactly to do each day. There is no guessing. Even the math involved is simple as you are simply taking the maximum weight you can do for a full routine and dividing it in half. It also allows for plenty of practice.

One of the routines is done 3 times a week.

Practice allows you the opportunity to become a better and more efficient lifter.

The 5x5 workout program places a large importance on building strength, which is why we are here. With this approach, you will build a bigger and stronger base.

Lastly, the 5x5 workout program does not use machines. It makes people get on their feet and trains them to lift heavy.

As with any workout, there are disadvantages as well. The simplicity factor mentioned earlier can also be looked upon negatively.

Typically intermediate and advanced lifters tend to need complexity in their training to continue to make gains.

Doing the 5x5 and adding 5 pounds each time will only work for so long before you need something else. If you can already rock a barbell, this will not work as well for you.

Seasoned lifters also need an increase in their training volume to gain size.

The StrongLifts 5x5 workout program does not provide this.

If a lifter is already strong it also does not offer adequate intensity to make them stronger.

There will come a time when a lifter needs to lift at approximately 90 percent of their 1RM or more to get stronger by doing sets of 3, 2, or 1 rep.

There are other variations to the 5x5 workout program. One of these is the Madcow 5x5 workout.

This is recommended when the StrongLifts 5x5 workout is no longer effective for your squat routine.

Your age and body weight are the big factors that determine when you are recommended to switch from StrongLifts to Madcow.

It is recommended that the heavier/ lighter you are the later/ sooner you switch.

You do the same workouts as you do in StrongLifts with 3 modifications that will enhance your recovery from the progressively stressful workouts.

You will now do ramped up sets which consist of increasing your weight with every set similar to when warm up and the end with an intense set of 1x5.

Rather than increasing your weights with each workout, you will now by increasing weekly by 5 pounds. This is because at the intermediate level, your body does not recover as quickly as when you were doing the beginning exercises.

Also rather than squatting heavy all 3 days a week, you will instead do a heavy squat the first day, then do a light squat for your next workout day, and finish your week with another heavy squat.

Workout 1: Squat 1x5, Bench Press 1x5, Barbell Rows 1x5
Workout 2: Squat 2x5, Overhead Press 1x5, Deadlift 1x5
Workout 3: Squat 1x3, Bench Press 1x3, Barbell Rows 1x5

Start light rather than heavy. While it is easy in the beginning you should focus on your technique and speed.

Another is the Texas Method 5x5 workout. It is based on three sessions a week lifting 5RM in four vital compound lifts which are the same as those from StrongLifts.

The five rep max should be approximately 85 percent of your 1 rep max. Ensure you use a spotter each time you work out.

The goal is to rapidly increase your strength. Make sure you are not rushing your sets and are resting for adequate amounts of time between each set. You should take approximately 2 minutes between each.

Maintain your schedule of having a rest day between your workouts. Make sure you warm up before each move and then lift approximately 90 percent of your 5RM. This will break down the maximum amount of muscle tissue.

When doing your deadlifts, only do one set of five because they are harder and if you do more, you will not be able to fully recover.

The second workout focuses on recovery. In this one, you will do 2 sets of 5 reps that are 80 percent of the weight of the first workout.

In your first 5x5 workout, you will be doing the Squats.

You will need to do 5 sets of 5 reps with the weight being 90 percent of your 5 RM's.

Then you will do your Bench Press, also being 5 sets of 5 reps and the weight is 90 percent of your 5 RM's.

Next, you will do your Deadlifts, this time only doing 1 set of 5 reps at 90 percent of your 5 RM's.

You will want to attempt to increase this every week.

The next routine is for intensity. The goal is to set a new five-rep max in each move with a 2.5-5 percent increase as the target.

Figure out what that is and then work up to it. If you aren't able to increase your 5RM during this workout, don't be disheartened.

Stick to the same weight for the next workout – one more week with it under your belt could make the difference.

Chapter 4: Leg Exercises

Forward Lunges

1. Start by setting your feet the width of your shoulders and arms on your hips.

2. Take a large step forward, keeping your back as straight as you can.

3. Lunge forward, making sure your front thigh is parallel with the ground and the back of your knee is as close to the floor as possible, but not quite reaching it.

4. Coming back to the standing position, you will next switch to the opposite.

5. Do 3 sets of 10 to 15 reps per side

NOTE: Both knees should be bent at 90-degree angles.

Backwards Lunges

1. Using a chair, place your feet close to the back of the chair so that when you step back it prevents your knees from going past your toes. Execute a standing abdominal brace by pulling your belly button a little towards your spine. Keep your spine as upright as possible.

2. With your right leg, step back and position the ball of your foot on the floor. Keep your hips facing forward. This will inhibit your body from twisting. Keep your spine straight and bend both knees to lower your body down. Only use the back of the chair for support if you need it.

3. Push into the floor with your left leg as you rise to the standing position. Repeat this movement for 30 seconds and then switch sides. To achieve maximum benefits, your movements should be slow and steady.

Olympic Lifts:

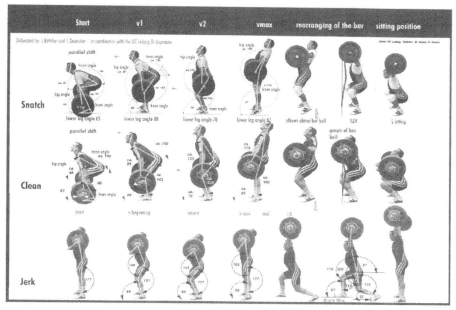

Consists of the snatch and the Power Clean. They take dedication proper technique to master. You will need to ensure you give this exercise your complete concentration on your body position and technique. You should only focus on one of them, not both.

Leg Press

This is great for beginners and it works the quadriceps.

Sitting on the machine, put your legs in front of you with your feet the same width as your shoulders. Gradually lower the safety bars holding the weighted platform in place and press the platform all the way up until your legs are completely extended in front of you.

Note: Ensure that you do not lock your knees. Your torso and the legs should make a perfect 90-degree angle. This is your starting position. As you breathe in, gradually lower the platform until your lower and upper legs make a 90-degree angle.

Using the quadriceps go back to the position you started in as you breathe out, pushing with the heels of your feet. Repeat for the amount of repetitions you want and ensure you lock the safety pins in place properly once you are done. You do not want the platform to fall on you while it is loaded with weights.

Chapter 5: Back Exercises

Deadlift: muscles worked- legs and upper back

1. Walk towards the bar, standing with the middle of your foot positioned under the bar. Do not have your shins touch it. Your feet should be hip-width apart with your toes pointed out 15 degrees.

2. Grasp the bar with your hands placed approximately the width of your shoulders and your arms should be vertical from the front view and hanging right outside your legs.

3. Your knees should be bent until your shins touch the bar. Do not move the bar. Keep it over the middle of your foot.

4. Elevate your chest and keep your back straight. Do not move the bar or have your hips drop. Also, do not squeeze your shoulder blades.

5. Pull. Inhale deeply, holding it while you stand up. Keep the bar against your legs. Don't shrug or lean back at the top.

Deadlift Form

o The bar should be vertically over the middle of your foot when looking from the side.

o The barbell should be on the floor, over the middle of your foot, at the start of each rep.

o Your heels should be hip-width apart, a little more constricted than on the Squat.

o Your foot should be entirely flat on the floor, toes turned so that they are approximately 15 degrees.

o Your grip should be narrow, approximately the width of your shoulders, with the bar close to your fingers.

o Your arms should appear to be vertical when looking from the front and appear slightly inclined from the side.

o You should keep your elbows locked prior to and throughout the pull, up until lockout. They should never be bent.

o Your chest should be elevated to avoid rounding your back. Do not squeeze your shoulder blades together.

- o Shoulders should be in front of the bar from the side view. Make sure you relax your shoulders and traps.

- o Shoulder blades should be over the middle of your foot when looking from the side

- o Your head should be aligned with the rest of your spine. Do not look up or look at your feet. Keep it straight, staring forward.

- o Your lower back should be neutral, with a small, natural arch. Do not round your back or have excess arching.

- o Hips should be set up to look like a half Squat and be higher than parallel. You should not Squat your Deadlifts.

- o The bar should be set up above the middle of your foot with your shoulder blades over the bar. There should be a straight line from your head to your lower back.

- o Inhale deeply at the bottom, holding it at the top. Breathe out and then back in at the bottom.

- o When pulling do not jerk the bar off the floor. Instead, pull it slowly while dragging it over your legs.

- o When lowering back down, put your hips back first and once the bar reaches your knees, bend your legs.

- o When you are between reps, you should not bounce. Instead, rest for a second or two, lift your chest, take a breath and pull again.

- o Let your traps be relaxed and hang. Do not roll or shrug your trap muscles at the top.

○ Always lock your hips and knees, making sure not to lean back at the top.

Bent-Over Barbell Deadlift

Hold the barbell with your palms facing down, bending your knees somewhat and bring your torso frontward, by bending at the waist, while you keep the back straight until it is nearly parallel to the floor.

Note: Ensure that you keep your head up. The barbell should hang straight in front of you as your arms hang perpendicular to your torso and the floor. This will be your starting position.

Now, keep your torso still, exhale and lift the barbell to you. Keep your elbows close to your body and only use your forearms to hold the weight. At the top constricted position, squeeze your back muscles and hold it there for a brief pause.

Then breathe in and gently lower the barbell back to the starting position.

Repeat for the desired amount of repetitions.

Chapter 6: Chest Exercises

Top 10 Chest Building Exercises

1. Dumbbell Squeeze Press

a. Lie down on a bench and hold a pair of dumbbells with your arms above your chest, palms facing each other.

Allow the weights to touch and squeeze them together as hard as you can.

Maintaining the squeeze, make sure the dumbbells stay in contact with each other.

Lower them to the sides of your chest.

Then push them upwards, back to the beginning position.

2. Barbell Flat Bench Press

a. Use this exercise at the beginning of your chest workout. For more complete chest development, vary the grip width.

b. Sit at the end of your bench and then lie down by lowering yourself back on the bench. Place your eyes underneath the bar.

c. Elevate your chest and tense your upper back. Place your shoulder blades down and back. Squeeze them.

d. Place your pinky finger on the inside of the rings. Hold the bar low and close to your wrist. Clasp the bar using the complete grip to prevent it from moving.

e. Set your feet flat on the floor in s stance that is approximately the width of your shoulders. One at a time, set your feet underneath your knees.

f. To lift the bar out of the rack, straighten your arms.

g. Place it where it is balanced over your shoulders by moving it horizontally.

3. Flat Bench Dumbbell Press:

Done at the beginning of your exercise routine for the day. Get into a steady lying back position on an exercise bench.

Rest your head, shoulders and buttocks on the bench, legs a little apart with your knees bent at 90-degree angles and your feet level on the floor.

Hold a dumbbell in each hand and positioned so that your palms are facing your feet.

You need to put your arms out straight so that they are supporting the dumbbells directly above your chest, and so that the dumbbells are touching each other.

Breathe in and hold your breath, when you are ready, as you lower the weights by bending your arms and keeping your elbows aimed out to the sides.

As you bring the dumbbells down, move them out to the side so that they will be beside your chest and shoulders in the bottom position.

As the dumbbells approach your chest, do not stop but promptly switch directions and push the dumbbells back up until you have completely put your arms out again.

Press the barbells up in an almost straight line directly above the chest. Forcefully breathe out as you pass the most challenging point on the ascent.

Pause in the top position with the dumbbells together and then repeat for any necessary repetitions.

You can also vary this by pausing in the bottom position. This is a more difficult alternative and necessitates a double breathing cycle for safety and efficiency and should be done as follows:

    i.   As you bring down the dumbbells, breathe out until you reach the bottom position then pause while preserving muscle tension, then inhale slightly more than normal and hold your breath as you push the dumbbells back up.

Breathe out after you pass the most challenging point on the way up and then pause briefly when the arms are completely extended. Then breathe in, holding your breath as you begin lowering the dumbbell and then gradually let your breath out as you approach the bottom position, and pause before repeating.

ii. When you breathe in and hold your breath, you help steady the chest, forming a firm base in which the muscles can tighten. It also stabilizes the trunk, giving you more stability in your basic position.

When you let your breath out, your body slackens and you lose the pressure in your chest cavity.

Breathing out should always be done when the muscles are not under maximum contraction.

4. **Incline Bench Cable Fly:** Do this exercise towards the end of your chest routine.

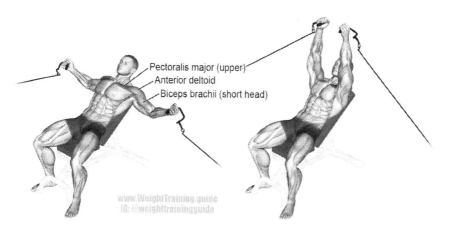

Pectoralis major (upper)
Anterior deltoid
Biceps brachii (short head)

www.WeightTraining.guide
IG: @weighttrainingguide

a. You should start with your hands to your sides with your elbows slightly bent.

b. Place an incline bench in the middle of two cable stacks in a cable crossover machine.

c. You need to set the cable pulleys to the lowest position and lie back on the bench. Next, you will take hold of the D- handles.

d. Begin with your hands straight out to the sides. They should be approximately shoulder height. Do not lock your elbows. They should be slightly bent.

e. As you contract your pecs, you will pull your hands up and together until the handles are almost touching. You should be maintaining the same bent elbow position throughout the exercise. Do not lock them or bend them further.

f. Your finishing position will be with your hands together directly above your chest. Once you are in the top position, you will want to contract your pec muscles a little more to maximize the contraction.

g. Do 3 or 4 sets consisting of 10 to 15 reps per set.

5. **Incline Dumbbell Pull-Over:** NOTE: this is not good for people with shoulder issues.

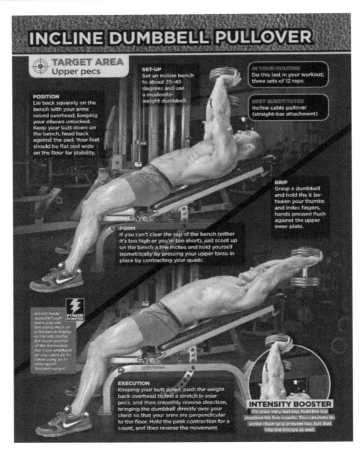

a. Lie on the bench so that only your shoulders are being supported.

b. Keep your feet flat on the floor, approximately the width of your shoulders.

c. Your head and neck will be hanging over the bench.

d. Your hips should be preferably at a somewhat lower angle than your shoulders

e. Hold the dumbbells with your hands positioned in a diamond (rhombus) shape using your thumbs and pointer fingers. Your palms need to be facing the ceiling.

f. The movement will start with the dumbbell over your chest and your elbows should be bent 10 to15 degrees. Do not change this at any point throughout your exercise.

g. Take inhale deeply and hold it while you slowly lower the weight backward over your head until your upper arms are aligned with your torso. They should be parallel to the floor.

h. The weight will travel in an arc-like motion towards the floor.

i. Breathe out and pull the dumbbell back so that it is directly over your chest again, purposely squeezing your chest muscles.

j. Hold for a brief second, and then repeat the exercise for at least 12 reps

6. Incline Dumbbell Press

a. Set the bench backrest to a 45-degree angle.

Hold a pair of dumbbells with your arms above your chest with your palms facing your feet.

Bring the dumbbells down to your chest level and then raise (press) them back up to the beginning position.

7. Low Incline Barbell Bench Press

a. The incline should also be the primary exercise in chest training for bodybuilders.

Bodybuilding prep should use the smith machine bar, incline dumbbell presses and the incline bar.

This cultivates the strength and build of the pectoral muscles (both the upper and middle regions) and front deltoids.

The upper pecs are hit exceptionally hard with the inclined angle of this press.

The main benefit in doing incline presses is to develop the upper portion of the pectoral muscles.

The muscles affected by this exercise are the upper chest, the triceps, and deltoids.

If you want to have a thick chest, it is extremely important for you to utilize the incline bar press.

Incline presses are an extremely widespread exercise in bodybuilding groups.

Some do them instead of flat bar bench press for building their chest.

b. How it is done:

   i. On an incline bench, lean back at approximately 30 to 45 degrees. Your feet need to be flat on the floor in order to give yourself a good, sturdy base.

   Your lower back should be flat against the bench.

   Slightly arch your back during this lift.

   ii. Grab the bar with a wide, medium grip.

   When you get the bar off of the rack, do not go down instantly with it. Raise the bar off of the rack and hold it for a second or two right above your head with your arms locked. This will help you to get oriented with it first.

   iii. Begin going down with the weight gradually until you touch the muscles directly below the point where the clavicles meet.

   In laymen's terms, this is essentially the upper chest or bottom of the chin.

Pause for a moment so that you do not bounce the weight off your chest, then raise it back up to the top position, breathing out on the way back up.

If you touch the nipple area, you went too low.

iv. The bar should be positioned so that it either touches your chin, or be just below your clavicle. Going even an inch too low takes the emphasis off the objective area.

You need to keep your wrists straight and your elbows below your wrists with your arms placed at a 45 degree angle.

Do not keep your elbows back because this puts maximum stretch on the pecs and severe stress on the shoulder joint.

8. Weighted Push Up

a. Get into the push-up position wearing a weighted vest.

This can also be done using a sandbag draped over your upper back or a weighted plate balanced on your upper back.

Your arms should be straight and hands should be placed a little wider apart than your shoulders.

Bend at the elbows and lower your body until your chest almost touches the floor.

Pause and then push your body back up.

9. Close Grip Bench Press

a. Use an overhand grip that is a little narrower than the width of your shoulders and hold the barbell above the sternum with your arms straightened.

Lower the bar to your chest and hold for 1 second.

Press the bar back up to the starting position.

10. Chest Squeeze Push Up

b. Place two dumbbells next to each other. You want
    to make sure they are touching and the handles are
    parallel to each other. Get into the standard push-
    up position.

    Each hand will grab a dumbbell handle. Keep your
    arms straight and your body should form a straight
    line, from ankles to head.

    Press the weights together forcefully. Lower your
    body until your chest almost touches the floor.

    Push your body back up to the starting position,
    ensuring that you do not stop squeezing the
    dumbbells together.

Breathing is not critical if you are using very light weights. It only becomes important when the muscles become fatigued or you are using heavy weights.

As the exercise becomes more challenging, your breathing becomes crucial.

When using dumbbells, you may find that you will need to use a little less weight than when handling a barbell.

This is due to the dumbbells being more challenging to control, particularly is one arm is weaker than the other.

This is why you should start with lifting weights that are lighter and slowly build up to the heavier weights.

When increasing the resistance gradually, you will also be strengthening the stabilizer muscles at the same time.

The stabilizer muscles hold your trunk and arms in place as you perform the movements.

This keeps the movements smooth and you will not have to experience extreme and unnecessary stress that happens when you are slightly off balance.

Muscular imbalances can be determined if using the barbell press. In order to keep the barbell consistently level, you need to compensate. There is no compromise when using dumbbells.

You could have one arm that is capable of lifting while your other arm cannot. If it is determined that there is an imbalance, you can take action to make the muscle strength in both arms equal to each other.

Sometimes people tend to push down with their feet to raise their hips when pushing the dumbbells upward.

This is especially true when they are heavy. You can change the trunk angle that you push the dumbbells upwards by raising your hips to bring in more of the sternal portion of the pecs.

These are generally stronger than the upper pectorals. You want to be careful not to raise the hips too much though because it creates more of an arch in the lower back which can cause injury if it becomes extreme and you are using heavy weights.

With a neutral grip, the dumbbell press can also be done. This is done by keeping your elbows pointed in the direction of your feet. You would only involve the upper portion of the pecs with the anterior deltoid but it also puts more stress on the triceps.

You bring in a deeper contraction of the pectorals and the anterior deltoid when you move the dumbbells in so that they touch in the higher position. This is a benefit that you do not get to achieve with a barbell.

There is an abduction in the shoulder joint in which the upper arms move vertically to the trunk to a position in front of and over the chest.

There is an abduction of the scapulae in which the muscles pull the scapulae from the spine in the direction of the ribs.

There is an extension in the elbow joint in which the forearms move away from the upper arms until they are fully extended.

The flat bench dumbbell press is extremely important in bodybuilding for complete development of the chest, particularly the middle section and frontal shoulder joint muscles. It is a support exercise for the serratus anterior and triceps.

The mixture of shoulder girdle abduction, shoulder joint horizontal flexion, and elbow extension is extremely important in all pushing, grabbing, and forward reaching actions. It can be seen in boxing when a person is performing a roundhouse or jabbing.

It can also be seen in football when a player is blocking, pushing or tackling.

In baseball and softball the dumbbell press is also important because of batting and when side- arm throwing.

In gymnastics it is important for the use of the parallel bars and rings and when doing floor exercises.

Chapter 7: Other Exercises

How to enhance your butt muscles

There are three muscles that make up the butt: the gluteus maximus, gluteus medius (G-med), and gluteus minimus (G-min). The primary muscle is the gluteus maximus (G-max) and is the largest muscle in the body. The function of the G-max is upper leg extension.

The functions of the G-med and G-min are similar. They move toward the thigh, stabilize the leg during the single support phase of running and internally (with a flexed hip) and externally (with an extended hip) rotate the thigh.

Barbell squats have the potential to make your butt bigger through stimulation if your butt has the potential to do so. Working on the glute muscles will give you a better chance of sculpting them.

Contrary to popular belief, constantly clenching your butt (perma-clenching) is not good for you. It leads to increased wear on your lumbar discs and sacroiliac joints, decreased core support, hip pain, and causes the pelvic floor to be too tight.

Exercise 1: Locating your G-max
  1. Stand.

  2. Place fingers on your sit bones. Tighten and hold for 20 seconds.

3. Release

Do this 10-15 times. Repeat hourly

<u>Exercise 2: Locating your Adductor Magnus</u>
1. Sit on a chair.

2. Make a fist, placing it between the knees and squeeze your knees together. Do this, holding the squeezing position, for 20 seconds.

3. Release

4. Repeat 10-15 times every hour while seated.

<u>Exercise 3: Locating your Hamstrings</u>
1. Sit on a chair.

2. Stretch out your legs with your feet in front of your knees.

3. Dig your heels into the floor.

4. Pull your feet in the direction of the chair without moving them. This will contract your hamstrings. Hold this position for 20 seconds and release.

*Repeat 10-15 times every hour while seated.

Squats: The Total Body Workout

Squats create total body strength, improve athleticism, and stimulate total body muscle growth. This is why they are considered royalty in the lifting world. The only problem is many people do not have enough mobility or ability to squat not only safely, but effectively as well.

You need mobility to achieve proper form and stability to control your movements through their intended range of motion.

5 Squat Mistakes

1. Not stretching or performing mobility work before you begin squatting. This should also be done throughout the week to increase flexibility.

    If your shoulders are tight, chances are when you use a barbell during your squat routine, all the weight ends up being pressed into your neck and you run the risk of compressing disks and pinching nerves.

    It will also cause a multitude of other problems such as pain in your neck, back, knees, and even your feet.

    To counteract and prevent this from happening, perform shoulder warm-ups to increase mobility and prevent injuries.

    For tight hips, perform air squats next to a pole to maintain proper form.

2. Stopping at 90 degrees. To build muscle, you need to go as low as possible for every rep. The lower you squat, the more you activate your glutes and hamstrings.

    Powerlifting stops just below 90 degrees. Body building requires going all the way down, known as Ass to Grass (ATG). This places the barbell directly above your hips for proper positioning.

3. You should be pressing through the middle of your foot and not your toes to finish your reps.

   You should be bending at your knees and hips at the same time as you go down. Then come back up to a standing position.

   If you break at one before the other, it causes your heels to come off the ground, putting more pressure on your toes. This can lead to foot injuries. Practice fluid movement without any weight first until you master proper positioning.

   If your knees are bending inward, stop immediately to correct. This can cause ACL tears. To correct this, you can widen your stance or slightly point your toes outward, as your knees will follow your toes.

4. Do not breathe during reps, as this will cause you to lose core stability and cause you to collapse.

   You want to keep that pressure in your core and keep your proper form. To do this, take a deep breath, keeping your core tight and flexing your abdominal muscles. Then hold your breath as you go down and come back up. Do not breathe out until you come up to the top of the movement.

5. You're not resting enough between your sets.

   For quality reps, you need to rest 2-3 minutes between sets to allow your body adequate recovery time.

   For a 1 rep max, you should rest 3-5 minutes. Beware of resting for too long. Resting for 10-15 minutes makes your body become tight and increases your risk of injuring yourself.

10 Ways to Boost Your Squat Routine

1. Train for Maximum Strength: You need a base of absolute strength.

2. Train for Power with Submaximal Reps: strength/ speed and speed/ strength. This can be done with speed squats.

3. Train Speed & Speed: strength. Jump squats are good for this.

4. Squat twice a week. For full recovery, allow 48-72 hours between sessions.

5. Train for Squat Depth: If you cannot maintain proper form because of a lack of core control, do not force a deep squat.

6. Do not forget about your front squats. The benefits of front squats include similar muscle activation as the back squat without as much joint compression and stress from using less weight, increased core stability which allows greater depth without compromised spinal position. This creates increased relative muscle activation with lighter weights than that with back squats.

7. Spread the Floor: Push your knees outward during squats to prevent valgus collapse. It will emphasize hip and

posterior chain development and increase your squat numbers.

8. Train the Purse: You need to be stable in the bottom position if squatting to depth. Use submaximal loads and squat to max depth while maintaining trunk integrity.

9. Bend the Bar: Engage the lats, create additional stability in the trunk, and provide a larger shelf for the barbell by driving your elbows down and back. You will also prevent the bar from jumping off your back during explosive squats which will improve your rep quality and decrease your chance of injury.

10. Rack at the Correct Height: The rack should be set up with the barbell set in the middle of the nipple and shoulder height. This is down low enough to permit you to squat to weight out and rack back in as well.

Proper Form
- Squat with your heels shoulder-width apart with your heels under your shoulders.
- Turn your feet out 30 degrees, keeping your whole foot flat on the floor. Don't raise your toes or heels.

- Drive your knees to the side, in the direction of your feet, locking your knees at the top of each rep.

- Bend your knees and hips at the same time. Shift your hips back and down while thrusting your knees out.

- Bend with a natural arch in your lower back like when you stand. No rounding or extra arching. Keep your back in a neutral position.

- Squeeze the bar fiercely but do not try to maintain heavy weight with your hands. Let your upper back support the bar.

- Use an average grip, thinner than when you Bench Press. Your hands should be further than the width of your shoulders.

- Place the bar in between your traps and rear shoulders, known as a low bar, or on your traps, known as the high bar. Then center the bar.

- Your wrists will hurt and bend if you try to brace the bar with your hands. Support it with your upper-back.

- Elbows should be at the back of your torso at the top, not vertically or horizontally. Align with your torso at the bottom of your Squat.

- Curve the upper portion of your back to establish support for the bar. Compress your shoulder blades and inflate your chest.

- Elevate your chest before you un-rack the bar. Keep it raised and firm by inhaling deeply before you Squat down.

- Keep your head aligned with your torso. Do not look at the ceiling or your feet. Also, do not turn your head to the right or left.

- Your back angle should always be diagonal, not vertical or horizontal. The precise back angle depends on your body type and the bar position.

- Place the bar on your back and put your feet under the bar. Remove it from the rack by straightening your legs. Walk back.

- On the way down, bend your hips and knees simultaneously. Hips should be back with the knees out, keeping your lower back neutral.

- Squat down until your hips are below your knees. If the thighs are parallel to the floor, it isn't far enough.

- Move your hips upright, keeping your knees out, your chest elevated and your head neutral.

- Between reps, stand with your hips and knees locked straight. Inhale and exhale while you get ready for the next rep.

- Lock your knees and hips. Step forward and hit the rack, bending your knees to place the bar on the rack again.

- Transport the bar in a vertical line above the middle of your foot. Do not perform any horizontal movements.

- At the top, take in a deep breath and hold it at the bottom. Breathe out at the top.

Active Squat/ Chair Pose

1. Stand.
2. Bend knees into the proper squat position.
3. Contract your G-max while holding for 30 seconds.
4. Contract your adductor magnus, holding for 30 seconds.
5. Contract your hamstrings, holding for 30 seconds.
6. Contract all three at the same time while holding for 30 seconds

This is great for decreasing lower back tension, fatigue from sitting for extended periods of time, and hip tightness.

***If you begin to experience any knee pain:

- Increase your standing height and only bend your knees a couple degrees
- Widen or narrow your feet position
- Lean against a wall to squat
- Use a rolled up towel to squeeze between your knees

Chapter 8: Recipes

Drinks
Bounce Back Smoothie

Prep takes about 5 minutes
Cook time takes about a minute
This serves 2 people

What's in it:

1 c. Almond Milk
1 tbsp. Honey
1 c. Spinach
3 med. Strawberries

½ c. Blueberries
1 med. Banana
2 tbsp. Greek Yogurt
1 scoop Protein Powder

Instructions:

1. Put all ingredients together in a blender.

2. Blend for 30 seconds.

Nutrition Facts
Number of Servings: 2

Amount Per Serving

Calories 227

Protein 20g

Carbs 30g

Fat 3g

Fiber 6g

Notice: Eating the right diet for your goals may result in increased gains and decreased bodyfat.

Lean and Green Meal Replacement Smoothie

What's in it:

.25 c. Water
.25 c. Pineapple
1 scoop Lean Body Natural Protein
.25 oz. Wheatgrass
3 Strawberries (raw or freshly frozen)
.33 Banana
.5 Small Avocado
1 c. Chopped Kale
Ice for thickness

Instructions:

1. Put all ingredients into a blender and blend until smooth.

2. You can freeze the fruit to chill the smoothie rather than using ice.
3. If you would like to add more complex carbs and make a thicker shake and make it more filling, add .25 cup of uncooked oatmeal.

Breakfast

<u>High Protein Cheeseburger Omelet</u>

Prep takes about 15 minutes   Cook Time takes about
10 minutes
This serves 1 person

What's in it?

2 lg Eggs
Salt & Pepper, as desired
.25 c. Egg Whites
Ketchup
2 tbsp. Reduced Fat Cheddar Cheese
Sliced Pickles
.25 c. Sliced Tomatoes

Any other toppings you wish
4 oz. Lean Ground Beef

Instructions:

1. Combine eggs and egg whites. Whisk.
2. Over medium heat, heat up skillet. Add eggs and cover.
3. Cook eggs until desired. Remove from heat.
4. Cook ground beef, salt, and pepper in a second skillet. When done, spread over one side of cooked eggs.
5. Top with tomato and pickle.
6. Fold eggs over beef.
7. Sprinkle cheese on top.
8. Cover and cook on low until cheese is somewhat melted.

Note: For a vegetarian-friendly dish, replace beef with tofu and cheese with soy crumbles.

Nutrition Facts

Amount Per Serving

Calories 409

Protein 50g

Carbs 12g

Fat 16g

Notice: Eating the right diet for your goals may result in increased gains and decreased bodyfat.

Lean Pro 8, Banana, Blueberry, and Oatmeal Pancakes

What's in it?

2 tsp baking powder
.5 cup blueberries
.5 medium banana
.5 cup oatmeal, uncooked
.5 cup egg whites (or 3 egg whites)
1 scoop Lean Pro 8

Instructions:

1. Put oatmeal in blender or food processor and blend. It should become a fine powder.

2. Add eggs, baking powder, banana, and protein powder. Blend on pulse until smooth.

3. Put blueberries in the mix and stir with a spatula or spoon.

4. Put skillet on med-high heat and measure approximately .125 cup or 2 tbsp. batter per pancake.

5. Cover pancakes with a lid while they cook to help the inside cook faster. Cook them for approximately 45 seconds to 1 minute on the first side, and then approximately 30 sec to 45 sec on the other side.

Nutrition Facts
Calories: 544
Fat: 11 g
Carbs: 64
Protein: 47 g

Dinner
Lean Beef Spinach Meatball Pasta

Prep takes between 5 and 10 minutes
Cook time takes about 10 to 12 minutes
This serves 1 person

What's needed for the meatballs?

Sea salt and pepper, to taste
.5 tbsp. cumin
1 tbsp. garlic, minced

.25 cup diced red onion
.5 cup shredded raw spinach
6 oz. lean ground beef

Ingredients for pasta:
2 oz wheat spinach pasta
1 tbsp low-fat parmesan cheese
5 cherry tomatoes
1.5 cup raw spinach
.125 cup marinara (natural, low sodium)

Instructions:

1. Preheat the oven to 405 degrees Fahrenheit.
2. Sauté red onions in skillet (for flavor) using coconut or olive oil.
3. Mix together the ground beef, red onion, shredded spinach, minced garlic, and spices.
4. Shape one or two meatballs approximately the size of your hands. Use a food scale if you would like them to be proportionate.
5. Set the meatballs on a baking sheet and place in preheated oven. Cook for 10 to 12 minutes.
6. Cook pasta. When done, mix in spinach, cheese, and tomatoes, as desired.

Nutrition Facts
Calories: 468
Fat: 6 g
Carbs: 50 g
Protein: 51 g

Snacks/ Desserts

Lean Body Gold Bar Banana Split with Protein Ice Cream

What's in it?

1 medium-large sized banana
1 tbsp. vanilla extract
.5 Lean Body Gold Bar (Caramel Peanut Protein Bar)
7 oz Greek yogurt
.5 scoop ISO LeanPro
Optional: 3 diced/ chopped strawberries

Instructions:

1. Put Lean Body Gold Bar in the refrigerator or freezer
2. Mix Greek yogurt, protein powder, and vanilla extract in a bowl. Whip until smooth.
3. Put bowl in refrigerator for 1.5 to 2 hours or until it is your desired firmness.
4. Slice banana vertically in half and place in separate bowl.
5. Put Lean Body Gold Bar in blender and pulse until it is broken into chunks.
6. Remove ice cream from freezer. Dig out the ice cream with an ice cream scoop and place on top of banana.
7. Sprinkle with the chunks of the Gold Bar and add fresh fruit, if desired.

NOTE: To increase the protein content, simply add 1 full scoop of protein. To add more carbs, use one full Lean Body Gold bar.

Nutrition Facts
Calories: 493
Fat: 12 g
Carbs: 49 g
Protein: 47 g

Chapter 9: Glossary

1RM: "One Repetition Max"; the maximum amount of weight that you can lift for a given exercise

Heavy Lifting: 85+ percent maximum effort for multiple sets of 1-5 reps

Hypertrophy: excessive development of an organ or part; particularly: increase in bulk (as by the thickening of muscle fibers) without multiplication of parts

Parkour: the activity or sport of moving rapidly through an area, typically in an urban environment, negotiating obstacles by running, jumping, and climbing.

Periodization: changing the program as you advance through the workout by challenging your muscles further each week and then having enough recovery time built in with an easier week so you do not become overtrained.

Perma-clenching: clenching your butt constantly

Traps: Short for trapezius. One of two large superficial muscles that extend longitudinally from the occipital bone to the lower thoracic vertebrae and laterally to the spine of the scapula (shoulder blade). Its functions are to move the scapulae and support the arm.

Valgus Collapse: when the knees buckle inward

Yoga: a Hindu spiritual and ascetic discipline, a part of which, including breath control, simple meditation, and the adoption of specific bodily postures, is widely practiced for health and relaxation.

Conclusion

Thank for making it through to the end of this book. I hope it was informative and able to provide you with all of the tools you need to achieve your strength training goals.

The next step is to start implementing what we have gone over into your daily routine. Make sure you are getting an adequate amount of rest as it is not only beneficial to your body normally, it also affects your strength training regimen.

You now know the basics of strength training and how to get started if you have never done anything like it before. This will then lead you into the 5x5 workout and some of the best workouts for your legs, chest, and back. Pick the ones that are right for you.

We have also discussed the royalty of strength training: the Squats. I have shown you some recipes that are ideal for all your nutritional needs so that you can come up with a meal plan during your exercise program.

As you research further, you may use the glossary for some of the terms you may not know so that you are able to easily reference those words as you work.

Every aspect has been covered for each workout to ensure you maximize your muscle mass and have fewer chances of injury. I have told you how to not only perform each workout, but also ensure you know the proper form for each.

Reference the pictures for each workout so that you are able to visually see how each workout should be properly done.

Please keep in mind the amount of reps you would like to perform to achieve your goals. 1 to 5 to build dense muscle and strength, 6-12 to build equal amounts of muscle strength and endurance and 12+ to build muscular endurance and size.

Finally, if you found this book useful in any way, a review on Amazon is always appreciated!

Body Weight Training

Get Bigger, Faster, and Stronger with Calisthenics

Table of Contents

There are no scenarios in which the publisher or the original author of this work can be in any fashion deemed liable for any hardship or damages that may befall them after undertaking information described herein.

Additionally, the information found on the following pages is intended for informational purposes only and should thus be considered, universal.

As befitting its nature, the information presented is without assurance regarding its continued validity or interim quality.

Trademarks that mentioned are done without written consent and can in no way be considered an endorsement from the trademark holder.

Introduction

Congratulations on downloading your personal copy of *Bodyweight Training*. Thank you for doing so.

The following chapters will cover the benefits of bodyweight exercises as well as beginner, intermediate, and advanced exercise routines.

The first chapter will also cover how different you will be in just 12 weeks.

There are plenty of books on this subject on the market, thanks again for choosing this one!

Every effort was made to ensure it is full of as much useful information as possible.

Please enjoy!

Chapter 1: 12 Weeks

If we lived in a perfect world, we could lose weight and fat instantaneously. Unfortunately this isn't how our body works.

Everything from the neurologic system to hormones can signal any change to your exercise routine and diet.

If you try to make a drastic change, like reducing calorie intake from 2,800 to 1,400 each day or take on an hour's worth of boot camp class at your first day back in the gym, the way your body chooses to adapt will do you more harm than good.

Your body will think that the food supply is short, you are beginning to starve, and it will start to save calories, and it will begin to burn protein to produce energy.

This shuts down the way the body burns fat and causes the downward spiral that will end up causing metabolic damage.

When you reduce calories, you are going to have to continue reducing calories. It's important that you stay away from this.

When you choose to try to reduce your intake of calories or your resting metabolic rate to lose weight fast, this will only cause rebound weight gain and not lasting weight loss.

Around two-thirds of people who lose weight this way will end up gaining all the weight they lost back and then some extra within a four or five year period.

The negative psychological impact that depriving yourself of food and pushing yourself during your workouts has on you isn't going to help you keep the weight off for any length of time.

If we look at the muscle and fitness side of this, diets that don't allow many calories can decrease the way your body is able to synthesize new, metabolically active muscle.

This makes your workouts useless. It will only end up making your workouts feel harder because you have less energy.

It's important to understand that your muscles do not become stronger while working out. You become stronger and more fit in the days and hours between your workouts when the muscles begin to adapt and repair themselves.

If you workout out for hours on end, or you're constantly working the same muscles groups, you're not allowing your muscles to recover. You're going to end up not seeing the results that you want.

Nothing is more frustrating than working super hard and then not being able to reap any rewards.

Generally, many people should only aim to lose about two pounds each week so they can maintain lean muscle. It varies from person to person as to how fast they are able to lose weight.

For those of you that haven't gone to the gym in over a year, and are the farthest from your goal, the quicker you will reach your goal.

Look at it this way: When you need to build more muscles and lose more weight, it will take less effort and time to challenge and improve your fitness.

When you start a new fitness routine, there are some people that will start noticing results before the pounds start coming off.

This is due to the reduction of eating processed food, refined carbs, and sodium and leads to a noticeable change in bloating within just a couple of days.

It isn't fat loss, but getting rid of the bloat gives a boost of motivation for most people. Significant muscle gain and weight loss take about eight weeks to set in.

However, the weight changes you experience aren't equivalent to all the benefits that are happing in your body.

If you want to drop a significant about of fat and gain muscles, eight weeks may only show a difference in your upper arms.

Local fat loss might actually be significant, but the increase in muscle keeps it from being noticed.

For a person that starts an eight-week program to lose around 20 pounds, any gain in muscle will show as definition instead of bulk because there isn't as much fat anymore.

A pound of muscle takes up more space than a pound of fat, so when people gain muscle while losing fat, they won't see as much of a reduction in body size.

For this reason, it is important that you pay attention, not only to your size and weight, but what your body fat percentage is to see a realistic look at how your body is changing.

A lot of the scales out there now will measure your weigh and body fat.

The improvements that you have with the strength and endurance of your cardiovascular system is going to be the best marker that you are becoming healthier.

If you ask a person why they don't work out, you will be hit with excuses like no time, not convenient, no membership, or don't understand how the machines work.

Bodyweight exercises get rid of these obstacles. You just need a small space.

It is relatively easy to squeeze in a workout wherever you might be.

Exercising without equipment could also be a stress reliever if you are working at home or traveling.

Every decade of your life, will lose about six pounds of lean muscle.

Research estimates that a person's metabolic rate will decrease around three to eight percent every decade after we turn 20.

This is what causes the decrease in muscle mass.

One of the best things that you can do to keep a strong metabolism and keep weight from adding up is to build more muscle mass.

When you stress your body with heavy loads, you will become stronger. It doesn't matter if it is just your body, weight machine, or dumbbells.

It honestly couldn't get any easier when you use your own weight to build strength.

You can customize it and do it anytime, anywhere.

You don't need a gym membership or equipment and takes less than 30 minutes.

If exercise machines, groups, treadmills, or free weights scare you, then your best bet would be bodyweight exercises so that you can get into a healthy routine.

So, how should you do bodyweight exercises? Cardio is beneficial, but building muscle is more important and is often overlooked.

Doing quick cardio sessions like combining burpees in the middle of movements of strength like a set of lunges or pushups will keep the heart swelling while improving strength and muscle development.

Very low, whole body aerobic training will improve fitness and muscle perseverance for females. Bodyweight exercises are one way to strength train.

Research tells that lean muscle mass has a great effect on your blood vessels, brain, hormones, lungs and heart.

Different studies link various forms of strength training to these benefits:

- Reduces the risk of strokes, cardiovascular mortality, and acute coronary syndrome

- Increased resting metabolic rate

- Increased insulin sensitivity

- Removes metabolic waste from muscles during rest

- Reduced bone and joint pain

- Increased oxygen usage by muscles

- More energy

- Better sleep

- Lower stress level

- Healthy blood pressure

- Healthy cholesterol level

- More lean muscles

Another benefit of bodyweight exercises is they are able to reverse the bad things that chronic dieting does to your body.

You think that diets are meant to help the body.

Yes, they are supposed to be helpful, but when somebody diets for years, they will often lose muscle tissue because of the low-calorie diet and the natural aging process.

The low calories don't supply the right amounts of nutrients to keep the muscles strong.

Muscles are essential to keep a healthy weight since they are metabolically active tissues that require more calories that fatty tissue needs.

How often should you train each week?

1. Perform exercises about two or three times each week. Each workout needs to use the big muscle group such as the core, chest, legs, and back to get the most out of the workout.

2. For every workout, try to do around eight or ten moves that work the muscles differently that you are working on. Perform each exercise in every set and perform eight to twelve reps of the exercise.

3. When you have completed your workouts, be sure to stretch about two to three days a week to keep from injuring yourself and to increase your range of motion, flexibility, and recovery.

It doesn't matter if your goal is weight loss or gain, just remember that you gain more benefits than how you look from bodyweight exercises.

The following are different ways that bodyweight exercises are able to help your immune, hormonal, cardiovascular, and cognitive health:

1. It is a very productive workout. Research has suggested bodyweight-based exercises like plyometrics give wonderful fitness results with short periods.

   Plyometric training will improve the voluntary activation and endurance with concentric, isometric, and eccentric contractions.

   Since there isn't any equipment, you can move from exercise to exercise more quickly so that you can reduce your rest time to maximize affects.

   You have heard about those brief but vigorous workouts that give big results.

   Eight weeks of conventional and high-intensity training improved fitness and reduced adiposity.

2. Helps to build and keep lean muscles.

   Building strength is an important part of keeping your metabolism strong as you get older because it increases your lean muscle mass that tends to decline as you age.

   Muscle mass plays an important part in maintaining metabolic functions and a healthy weight.

   It can help with hormonal balance, insulin sensitivity, and thyroid function.

   Your metabolic rate relies on how much lean muscle you have. This all means you are going to need extra calories to keep your weight.

   Have you ever noticed that muscular athletes are able to eat their weight in food?

This is because they have to train for many hours every day and the muscles they have burn off more calories than fat does.

Muscles are able to burn fat constantly, whether active or resting.

Your growth hormone production increases with bodyweight exercises.

People like to call your growth hormone the fountain of youth since they have fat burning abilities and help keep lean body mass.

If you just like cardio workouts like swimming or running more than strength training, listen to this: Lifting weights will give you more strength and performance that provides power for different exercises.

Building strength in the core or back is useful when you run or while strengthening the shoulders for swimming.

Just a couple minutes of bodyweight training has a huge effect on the metabolism of the body.

You may have heard about the "after burn" effect and know that when your exercising is finished that your body could still burn calories for many hours.

Just doing a 45-minute exercise routine can increase your metabolic rate for up to 14 hours.

3. Improves heart health.

   Exercise makes the heart pump blood more efficiently.

   This will help your circulation and blood pressure.

   The heart becomes stronger just like any other muscle, when it has to work under pressure.

   Strength training is tied to getting healthier cholesterol levels which reduces the risk of strokes or heart attacks.

   Longevity is also associated with regular strength building exercises.

   Patients that have had heart attacks are told they should start doing weekly resistance training to build up their hearts' strength.

4. Reduces the risk for diabetes.

   Exercise can naturally help diabetes because it takes glucose from the blood.

   It tells the glucose to move into the muscles where it is stored as glycogen and used as energy later.

   It keeps glucose from building up in the bloodstream.

   Over time, a buildup of glucose can damage tissues, blood vessels, and organs.

5. Improves moods and fights depression.

   Exercise is often referred to as a natural Prozac because it helps to reduces stress and improves

self-esteem, emotional health, sleep, confidence, and the ability to solve problems.

Endorphins are released when you exercise, and that causes a natural lift in your mood. It can help with depression and improve energy levels naturally.

6. Helps to maintain cognitive function.

    When you exercise, you reduce DNA damage because of the anti-aging effects of muscles and longevity. BDNF, a hormone, is stimulated when you exercise.

    This will then help your brain cells to regenerate. Exercise will lower inflammation and oxidative stress that is tied to disorders such as dementia and Alzheimer's.

7. Improves the health of bones and joints.

    Increasing the muscle mass will protect bones and joints, since strong muscles mean that you don't have to rely on your joints when you move.

    Exercising is able to help pain you may have in your hips, ankles, knees, and back while also increasing your bone density and strength.

    Exercising also helps to protect your frame and increase how your body fortifies bone reserves.

    This is critical to help prevent fractures, falls, and bone loss as we get older.

    Not everybody that exercises regularly ends up with sore muscles and joints that aren't flexible.

Bodyweight exercises are able to help with flexibility and strength.

When you use your full range of motion in bodyweight exercises, you are allowing your joints to move freely.

It also helps to improve your posture and can reduce injuries due to exercises.

8. You will gain strength in your core. Your core is not just your abs. 29 muscles make up the torso, and simple movements are able to engage them all.

   You won't get tighter abs with these movements, but your posture will improve. It can also relieve lower back pain, and improve your overall performance.

9. It is challenging for any level of fitness.

   Bodyweight exercises are easily modified to make them easier or harder to perform.

   Just by adding more reps, doing the exercises slower or faster, taking shorter or longer breaks, or adding movements like clapping after every pushup, are ways to make an easy workout a bit tougher.

   With each modification, the progress is obvious.

10. Your balance will become better.

    With this type of training, if you can increase your resistance means that you will increase your balance, as well.

A normal squat can be made harder by doing a pistol, or single-leg squat.

Movements such as that can help balance by increased control and body awareness.

11. You won't be bored. It is easy to get stuck in a rut with bench presses, lateral pull-downs, bicep curls, and treadmills.

    This is why bodyweight training is so exciting: There are numerous variations that could mix up any routine.

    Working with different exercises doesn't just relieve boredom, it's able to create progress and break through plateaus.

12. Changing an exercise is super easy.

    Exercising indoors isn't for everybody.

    Good news, you are able to do this alone, with a friend, inside, or outside.

    Add some strength moves to your next run in the park. Finish a swim in the pool with a bodyweight circuit to shake things up.

13. It helps prevent injuries. Injury is the main reason people stop working out.

    Preventing injuries is the top priority.

    Bodyweight training is safer for everybody.

    It doesn't matter their fitness level, age, or experience.

    Many movements could be effective for rehabilitation, even if you suffer from impairment.

Bodyweight supported gait walking and training in stroke patients has been very effective with their rehabilitation.

Bodyweight Exercises Versus Weight Machines

The main reason that most women avoid weight training is it seems intimidating.

Weight machines or free weights will provide you with the exact same benefits as bodyweight exercises because it all builds strength.

But they require you to buy equipment and have knowledge of the equipment in order to use it properly.

This sometimes means hiring a trainer.

It is believed that weight machines don't allow you to use your full range of motion and only works one muscle group at a time.

When you use free weights with bodyweight exercises it helps to work more muscles at the same time.

Bodyweight exercises are more accessible to the new strength trainer because they are modifiable and convenient.

All you will need is space and your body to perform them.

They are simple enough to do without supervision and still be safe from injuries.

It's more forgiving when you use your body and gives you the ability to adjust your workouts to your ability as compared to using machines or free weights.

A lot of women are afraid of lifting weights because they think it will end up making them look masculine.

You may be afraid that by focusing on strength training instead of burning calories will cause you to bulk up. That's not true. **The female body will get leaner, stronger, and more toned.**

Women don't gain muscles like mean do.

Most of the time, the female body will become tighter and smaller when they add strength training to their workout routine.

Fat will be lost and the muscle they gain will take up less space than the fat did, even though it does weigh more.

What about cardio workouts that are aimed towards calorie burning? How do they stand up to strength or bodyweight training?

Building muscles helps to speed up your metabolism, cardio exercises don't have that effect.

If you do too much cardio work without proper rest, it can actually slow down your metabolism.

Long cardio sessions can cause joint damage oxidative stress.

This can lead to illness, pain, and injuries.

Steady-state cardio such as cycling, swimming, or running helps to improve stamina, heart health, and endurance while cutting down on stress.

If used with strength training, it can cause muscle wasting caused by overtraining or aging.

This has the ability to depress the immune system and cause an increase in cortisol levels, which inflames the body.

Research has found that adults who do cardio regularly, like runners, could maintain fitness from aerobic activity.

They can also lose some muscle from the areas that aren't trained.

With a runner, their muscle will likely not change and they will only be able to carry strength in their legs.

The muscle mass in their arms and core will decrease.

Long-term cardio might have other effects with time like neurotransmitter function, altering hormone levels, bone loss, or joint wear-out.

Is there something better?

Sure, build up the muscles in the entire body, but prevent injuries, burn-out, or boredom by changing bodyweight or strength training with cardio workouts.

Can You Lose Weight By Using Bodyweight Training?

Short answer, yes and no.

Everybody will respond differently when they start to exercise.

Things like sleep, stress levels, and diet all have an effect on determining if you will or will not lose weight fast or at all.

Adding in bodyweight exercises to your normal routine can provide you with better results than cardio alone.

They will end up making you leaner than not exercising.

Research has found that steady-state cardio has a lower fat-burning and metabolic potential than strength-training does.

Muscle growth helps with fat metabolism and is able to lower your cortisol levels.

Cortisol is typically higher in people that are always stressed. Insulin is repaired when you lower your cortisol levels, and this will boost your body's natural fat-burning abilities.

Also, you may be able to get a handle on your cravings and food intake when you build strength instead of only burning calories.

When you over train on cardio workouts, it will likely cause you to become hungry.

This tells us that long aerobic exercises can work against weight loss.

Research has found that many people tend to eat more to compensate for the calories they are burning, but they found that strength training doesn't have that effect.

Even if you do become hungry while building muscles, your muscles need more calories to help them grow.

A woman with more muscle tone will develop an hourglass figure by adding shape to the legs and glutes, slim the waist, and tighten the stomach.

Even though bodyweight exercises don't create a huge reduction on the scale, they are going to change how you feel and look.

Eating enough to sustain body weight while exercising will help to prevent your body from going into starvation mode.

Starvation mode happens when you create a calorie deficit while losing weight.

The negative side effect of eating less and exercising more is that if you are stressed out plus you are exercising a lot, the body will likely slow down the thyroid.

When the thyroid works slowly, you will have difficulty maintaining your weight because your thyroid hormones play a crucial part in your metabolism.

How to See Results Quickly

Use the following steps to help safely speed up your weight loss goals.

1.   Intensify your workouts and increase protein intake.

     The combo of increased protein and exercise will help you to build muscle and burn fat while you cut calories.

     You can reduce your calorie intake as well as increasing your protein, so you won't lose muscle mass during your weight loss.

2. You must eat to give your body fuel.

   Every person needs different amounts of calories.

   Caloric deficits mean you burn more calories than you take in, which leads to weight loss, but a large deficit can create fat retention.

   A caloric surplus means you are eating a larger amount of calories than you burn, which is an ideal condition to build muscles.

   Don't get hung up on doing caloric math but just look at food as fuel.

   Pay attention to your body so that you know when it's hungry and eat whole foods that will fill you up on fiber, prevent fat storage and too much insulin secretion, and get you to your fat-loss goal.

3. Make strength training a priority over traditional cardio.

   Strength training is able to increase your calorie burn, even while you are resting, for 72 hours after you stop your workout.
   It also boosts the metabolism.

4. Recover. Give yourself a complete day each week to rest.

   Don't train the same muscles twice in a three-day period. Change up your intensity and workouts so that your body is able to recover.

It is normal to feel sore between one and two days after your workout, especially when you are just starting, but you should not feel like you can't walk or move.

5. Change things around every six to twelve weeks.

    To keep your body from hitting plateaus and adapting, you need to vary your workout.

    This might mean changing your rep sets, taking a spin class a few times a week, or doing a different swim stroke.

    If you don't, your body may adapt to the workout so much that it won't receive any benefits from it.

Chapter 2: Beginners

Do the words dragon flags, pistol squats, and one-armed pushups sound scary to you?

Maybe you don't have any experience with bodyweight or strength training and you're looking for some place to start.

That's what we're going to cover in this first chapter.

When you don't have any experience with any sort of exercise programs, the important thing is to create a new habit of exercising.

Bodyweight training may be one of the easier and simplest ways to exercise; there is a little bit of an infrastructure that you have to establish.

1. Come up with a routine.
2. Figure out how you want to track your progress.
3. Schedule times to work out.
4. Figure out where you are going to work out.

I'm going to try to help you work through all of these.

Number two is easy, all you really need is a notebook that you keep with you when you workout.

Three and four you will have to figure out completely on your own.

Number one should be easy after you finish this book.

All you have to do, really, is pick the workouts you like the best and do them at least three times a week.

For the best results, try to workout at the same time and in the same place.

This place and time should be an easy choice.

This means that you should pick an area that is most convenient.

This could be at home, at a park, or at a gym.

The only equipment that will show up in the workouts is a jump rope, pull up bar, dip bars, and a chair.

The jump rope and chair are easy, for the other two, you can come up with alternatives or purchase one.

Make sure you also pick the time that is most convenient.

For the most part, you're only going to work out for 30 minutes, three times a week.

Are you able to wake up 30 minutes earlier to work out first thing in the morning?

And are you actually going to work out each morning?

You have to be completely honest with yourself.

If you can't work out in the morning, that's perfectly fine.

Everybody dreams of being that person that wakes up bright eyed and bushy tailed ready to do jumping jacks and sit-ups, but that's not the truth.

I have personally tried to do morning workouts, but after a few days, I stopped.

It's not for me. I do better at night.

Make sure you don't make it optional. Don't ask "should I exercise?"

Tell yourself you're going to and view it as an appointment.

As a newbie, you are able to mix together simple moves to create a significant routine.

You don't have to do anything fancy as a beginner to see the results.

There are four main moves that, even if you are an intermediate, give you the best results.

- Supermans
- Squats
- Bodyweight Rows
- Pushups

These four moves will train your pulling and push strength, work your legs, and help your posterior stability.

You're probably wondering why there isn't a core exercise listed. That's because when you perform these moves with correct form, you will be working your core muscles.

Also, don't worry if you can't do a pushup or some of the other moves.

When you start out, begin with an easier or modified version of the exercise.

If you're not able to do a pushup, choose an elevated surface to place your hands on.

This could be just a few blocks, the back of your couch, or the wall.

Make sure it's not too easy though, it does need to be a challenging, but you need to be able to perform it properly.

If you find regular pushups too easy, elevate your feet.

Place your feet on some blocks to increase the difficulty.

Make sure that you always have your body in a straight line whenever you are doing a pushup, no matter if you have your hands or feet elevated.

Elbows also shouldn't flare out but should be close to your body.

Bodyweight rows look like a horizontal pull up.

You can use rings or pull up bar.

With your feet out, and gripping the bar, pull your chest towards the bar.

If you find a regular bodyweight row too hard, pick a higher bar.

If you find them too easy, then you should try elevating your feet. Your body should also be in a straight line when performing this exercise.

For squats, all you do is squat down as if you are going to sit in a chair; making sure your knees stay above your ankles.

If regular bodyweight squats are too hard, try sitting on a bench or chair and then immediately stand back up.

Once regular squats get too easy, start doing ass-to-grass squats, and when that gets easy, do prisoner squats.

If those squats become easy, try doing Cossack squats.

Some people confuse these for side lunges, but there is a big difference.

For a Cossack squat, start by doing a side lunge and then lower over further, your calf and hamstring should touch.

Do every rep on one side and then do it on the other side.

For the superman exercise, lay on your stomach and engage your lower back muscles and lift your legs and arms up off the ground.

If this is too hard, spread your arms and legs to the side as far as you can.

With supermans, you typically hold it for as long as you can.

There are some workouts, though, that tell you to do a certain number of reps.

The secret to success is progressing your workouts.

When something gets easy, don't just do more reps; make it a little bit harder.

Those people that you see doing handstand pushups aren't just superhuman; they worked their way up to that.

Beginner Moves

Squat: Start in a standing position with your hands out in front or behind your head. Start to push hips backward and squat down as low as you can go.

Your knees should not move forward or backward. Once you squat down, push yourself back up. The weight should be located in your heels and not your toes.

Variations of the squat are sumo: where you have you legs positioned about shoulder width, and plie: where your legs are shoulder width apart, and your feet turned out.

Pull Up: Stand at a pull up bar or rings. Grasp the bar or rings with hands, palms facing forward. Engage your muscles and pull yourself up until your chin is above the bar.

Lunges: Standing, with your arms by your side, step forward with your right leg and lower down.

The front knee should stay above the ankle and never move forward.

The back knee should move straight towards the ground.

Oblique Reaches: Lay on the ground with feet flat on the floor and hip width apart.

Extend your arms by your side and lift your head slightly.

Engage your oblique muscles and bend to touch your right fingers to your right heel, straighten, and repeat on the other side.

Fire Hydrant: Begin on your hands and knees. Raise one leg sideways, keeping your leg bent at a 90 degree angle.

Bird Dogs: Begin on hands and knees. Reach opposite arm and leg, bring back down, and repeat with the other side.

Side Plank: On one side, raise yourself up onto your forearm. The elbow should be directly beneath the shoulder. The legs should be stacked. The body should form a straight line.

Donkey Kicks: Begin on hands and knees. Raise one foot up towards the ceiling, keeping your knee bent at a 90 degree angle. Lower the leg back down and repeat.

Fingers to Toe Lifts: While standing, lift your right foot to your left hand and touch your fingers to the foot. Bring the foot back down and repeat on the other side.

Pulse Ups: Lying on your back, lift your legs straight up with your feet towards the ceiling. Gently pulse your feet towards the ceiling.

Windshield Wipers: Lying on your back with your arms straight out to the sides.

Raise your legs up with your feet pointing towards the ceiling.

Lower the legs down to the right, raise them back up, and then lower them to the left, repeat.

Speed Skaters: From standing, jump to the right and bring your left foot behind you and your left arm across your chest. Repeat this to the left.

Chapter 3: Beginner Exercises

100 Workouts
This workout looks harder than it is. You will be doing 100 reps, and you only have to do one set.

- 20 Leg Raises: 2 sets of 10
- 20 Crunches: 2 sets of 10
- 20 Tricep Dips: 4 sets of 5
- 20 Pushups: 4 sets of 5
- 20 Jump Squats: 2 sets of 10

Basic
Depending on your skill level, perform two to four sets of this workout. Try to keep from rest between exercises, but take a 60-second rest after each set.

- 50 Jumping Jacks
- 25 Squats
- 15 Pushups
- 30 Lunges, 15 on each side
- 30 Bicycle Crunches
- 60 Second Plank

Easy Full Body
Each exercise will provide you with how many sets you need to do before you move onto the next workout. Rest for a couple of minutes between each individual exercise, try to avoid resting between exercise sets, though.

- 40 Jumping Jacks, 1 Set
- 20 Squats, 2 Sets
- 8 Walking Lunges, 2 Sets
- 15 Crunches, 2 Sets
- 15 Knee Pushups, 2 Sets
- 20 Lying Oblique Reach, alternating sides, 2 Sets
- 30 Second Plank, 2 Sets
- 25 Fire Hydrants, 2 Sets
- 20 Bird Dogs, alternating legs, 2 Sets
- 30 Side Leg Lifts, each side, 2 Sets
- 25 Second Side Plank, 2 Sets

Five Minute Workout
This is a quick workout when you only have five minutes to get a workout in. Do three sets of this workout.

- 10 Knee Pushups
- 45 Second High Knees
- 10 Squats

10 Minute Workout
When you have a few extra minutes in your day, throw in this workout to get your blood pumping. Do this circuit three times.

- 1 Minute Cross Punches
- 10 Glute Bridges
- 1 Minute Hamstring Curls, alternating legs
- 10 Tricep Dips

15 Minute Workout
To get a better cardio workout, try this workout when you have 15 minutes. Do four sets of this circuit.

- 30 Second Forearm Plank
- 1 Minute Side to Side Shuffle
- 20 Forward Lunges, alternating legs
- 1 Minute Pivot and Reach

20 Minute Workout

For a full workout, and to really get your blood pumping, try this one out for size. Do five sets of this circuit.

- 20 Knee Pushups
- 1 Minute Curtsy Lunge
- 20 Lying Leg Curls, alternating legs
- 1 Minute Jumping Jacks

Butt Lifting Workout

For this exercise, you will be focusing on your glute muscles. Perform three sets of this circuit.

- 8 Modified Pistol Squats
- 8 Pulsing Plie Squats
- 8 One-Legged Plank Bridge, each leg
- 8 Supermans
- 8 Donkey Kicks, each leg

Cardio and Core

Perform the exercises as they say. Do all the sets for one exercise before moving to the next. Take a two-minute break between individual exercises.

- 60 Second Jump Rope, 3 Sets
- 40 Second Crunches, 3 Sets
- 30 Second Pulse Ups, 3 Sets
- 60 Second Fingers to Toe Lifts, 3 Sets
- 60 Second Standing Mountain Climbers, 3 Sets

- 30 Second Lying Oblique Reach, 3 Sets
- 45 Second Inchworm, 3 Sets
- 30 Second Superman, 3 Sets
- 20 Second Side Plank, each side, 3 Sets

Sweet At Home

There are three circuits in the workout. Repeat each circuit twice and then move onto the next circuit. Rest 30 seconds between each circuit set, and two minutes between each circuit.

Circuit One

- 20 Squats
- 20 Pushups
- 20 Jumping Jacks

Circuit Two

- 60 Second Plank with Alternating Leg Lift
- 15 Tricep Cips
- 20 Lunges

Circuit Three

- 20 Bicycle Crunches
- 30 Second Wall Sit
- 15 Squat Jumps

Toned and Cardio

Each exercise will be performed in three sets. Perform all sets before you move onto the next exercise. Rest a minute between each exercise.

- 60 Second Inchworm, 3 Sets

- 30 Second Side Plank, each side, 3 Sets
- 60 Second Standing Side Crunches, 3 Sets
- 60 Second Russian Twist, 3 Sets
- 45 Second Spiderman Plank, 3 Sets
- 30 Second Donkey Kick, each side, 3 Sets
- 45 Second Windshield Wipers, 3 Sets
- 45 Second Crunches, 3 Sets
- 60 Second Crab Kick, 3 Sets
- 45 Second Shoulder Taps, 3 Sets

5 – 10 – 15 (Workout)
For this workout, you will repeat the whole circuit five times:

- 5 Pushups
- 10 Sit Ups
- 15 Squats
- 10 Second Rest
- 5 Jump Squats
- 10 Alternating Lunges
- 15 Reverse Crunches

20 Minute HIIT
Repeat each circuit three times before you move onto the next circuit. Rest for a minute between each circuit.

Circuit One

- 30 Second Jump Squats
- 10 Second Rest
- 30 Second High Knees
- 10 Second Rest

Circuit Two

- 30 Second Pushups
- 15 Second Rest
- 1 Minute Wall Sit
- 15 Second Rest

Circuit Three

- 30 Second Mountain Climbers
- 10 Second Rest
- 30 Second Jump Lunges
- 10 Second Rest

Hear Pumper

You only have to do this workout in one set.

- 10 High Knees, each leg
- 2 Star Jumps
- 5 Plank Jacks
- 10 Mountain Climbers
- 20 Butt Kickers, each leg
- 15 Second Jump Rope
- 1 Burpee
- 20 Speed Skaters
- 1 Squat Jump
- 10 Jumping Jacks

Beginner Butt

Each exercise in this workout should be done four times. Rest for two minutes before moving onto the next exercise.

- 15 Squats
- 30 Donkey Kicks

- 30 Fire Hydrants
- 30 Second Wall Sit
- 15 Bridges
- 30 Side Leg Raises

Legs and Core

This is probably the hardest beginner workout, but you have complete control over this one.

Begin by setting a six-minute timer and try to do as many sets of the first three exercises as you can.

Try to rest as little as possible between each exercise. Then set another six-minute timer and do the same for the last three exercises.

Make sure you don't start out going too fast. Otherwise, you are going to get winded earlier on and struggle to finish. Go at a steady pace, and if you feel like you can speed up, then do so.

Circuit

- 10 Forward Lunges
- 15 Mountain Climbers, each side
- 10 Sumo Squats
- 10 Side Lunges
- 15 Shoulder Tap Planks, each side
- 10 Burpee

Chapter 4: Intermediates

We have talked about the benefits of bodyweight exercises. You don't need any equipment.

Bodyweight workouts can improve power, speed, athletic performance, burn fat, and build muscle.

By adding a jumping element you take the intensity up a level and it becomes a plyometric move.

Plyometric training isn't intended for newbies or anyone that has recently experienced an injury.

You need to have good form and focus when performing these exercises. That's why it's important to do these types of workouts before you tire and your performances slacks.

If you've never done a plyo workout before, you should only focus on three or four exercises first in your workout after your warm-up.

Perform two to three sets with three to five repetitions in each set. Do this at least two but no more than four times each week.

Give yourself two to three days to between plyo sessions. Even if you cannot do all of that, you will still receive some of the plyo benefit.

Training moderately with plyometrices a couple of times a week is effective in creating strength and power.

Remember, you don't have to purchase anything special for this.

Intermediate Moves

Plyo Pushup: Perform your regular pushup, but when you push back up, add more strength so that your hands come up and you clap before coming back down.

If you can't do it in full pushup, then try it in a modified pushup position.

Squat Thrusters: Begin in high plank, move your feet forward into a wide squat and bring your hands into a prayer pose.

Make sure your back stays straight, keep your shoulders down, and the chest out while you are in the squat position.

Pause and then bring your hands back to the ground and jump back into the high plank. Do this as quickly as you can.

Plyo Lateral Lunge: Stand with your feet together and your arms by your side. Engage your abs, send back your hips, and take a right step with your right foot.
Bend the right knee while keeping the left leg vertical while you lower into a lunge.

To help your balance, place your hands out to the side or in prayer position.

In one move, push with your right foot and hop to where your left was and send the left leg out to the side and into a lunge on the left side.
If it helps, picture it as a side step with a hop.
Repeat, alternating sides each time.

Reverse Lunge with Knee-Up:
Place your feet as wide as your hips and step backwards with your right leg. Lower yourself into a reverse lunge. Move your weight to the left foot.

Make sure your glutes and abs are engaged.

Bring your right leg forward, and, at the same time, jump on your left foot and raise your right knee to your chest.
Make sure you land gently on your left foot and then repeat the move.

Do all reps on one leg before moving to the other side.

Box Drill: This move works the calves. Begin standing on your right foot with the knee bent slightly. Your arms should stay loose at your side so that you can keep your balance.

Hop to the right, staying on the right foot. Staying on your right foot, hop to the left. Now hop to the front and then to the back. Switch to the left leg and reverse the direction. Try to do quick and small jumps.

For an easier variation: Do this exercise with both feet and try to build more speed as you jump.

Frog Squat Jump: Place your feet slightly wider than hip width and turn out your toes. Drop into a deep squat and allow your hands to touch the floor. Jump up like a frog would.

Keep your landing on the balls of your feet and repeat this movement as quickly as you can, and try to get higher each time.

Long Jump: Place your feet hip width apart. Crouch down into a squat with your arms behind you. Jump forward with your feet together, swinging your arms so that you keep your balance and land on your feet with your knees slightly bent.

If you have the space, continue to jump forward, or turn around and then jump back to where you were. Try not to rest between jumps.

Burpees with a Tuck Jump: Perform a normal burpee. Once standing, don't perform the normal jump. Instead, bring your knees up as high as you can and tuck the knees towards your chest. Land softly and continue into your next burpee.

Alternating Lunge Jumps: Begin by stepping forward with your right foot into a low lunge. Engage your abs and keep your right knee above the right ankle. Shift all of your weight to the right foot and jump.

Switch your leg position while in the air so that you land with your left foot in front and the right foot in back. Drop back into a low lunge and repeat. Think about height not speed.

Tuck Jumps: Place your feet shoulder width apart. Keep your knees bent and your hips back. Jump as high as possible and bring your knees up to your chest. Land softly on toes in the starting position. Keep jumping and avoid resting if you can.

Judo Roll with Jump: While lying on your back, tuck your knees into your chest with your ankles crossed. Engage your abs and roll yourself up into a seated position and rest your left foot on the ground.

Using your core, come to a standing position on your left foot. Lower yourself back to the start position and switch your feet.

For a modified version: Push yourself up with your hands and get your balance before jumping up. You can also use both feet to do the jump up.

Kneeling Jump Squat: Start by kneeling with legs spread slightly wider than your hips.

Take your arms behind you and swing them to the front to help you get the momentum to jump to a squat position on both feet.

Step the right foot backwards to come down onto your right knee. Bring your left foot back so that you are on both knees and then lower yourself back to the starting position.

Full-Body Plyometric Pushup: This is doing a regular pushup except your elbows are at a 90-degree angle. Push up as hard as you can so that you are momentarily floating.

Keep the core tight, so your hips don't drop as you land back into a high plank. Continue onto the next rep. To modify this: Master the plyo pushup that we covered earlier.

Single-Leg Deadlift into Jump: Stand on your left leg with you knee bent. Bend forward at the hips and let the right leg move up behind you until the right leg and chest are parallel to the floor.

In a single movement, swing your arms forward, let your chest rise, and push off the floor with your left foot. Move your right knee to your chest.

Gently step with your left foot and quickly lower back into the bent over position. Make sure you keep your right foot off the ground the whole time.

To make this easier: After you have landed, tap your opposite toe on the ground to help maintain your balance. You can also place your fingertips on the ground while your leg is behind you.

Horizontal Jump to Tuck Jump: Place your feet together. Bend your knees slightly and then push of the ground, jumping to the right as far as you can.

When you land, do a tuck jump. Now push off again and jump to the left. When you land, jump into a tuck jump. Repeat and alternate sides.

Pistol Squat Roll with Jump: Stand on your left leg with the knee slightly bent, and your right foot off the ground and stretched in front of you.

Balance your weight on your left foot, engage your core, rotate the hips back and slowly lower yourself into a low pistol squat. For your balance, extend your arms forward. Hold yourself in the squat.

Drop your butt to the ground and rock slightly on your back. Roll your weight back onto your left foot and stand, jumping as high as you can. Softly land and repeat.

Plyometric Pushup to Squat: Begin in a normal pushup position. Push up has hard as you can and generate some momentum. When you raise up, tuck your knees into your chest and take your feet under your body. You should be in a deep squat. Hold for a moment and then jump into a pushup and repeat.

Side to Side Shuffle: With knees slightly bent, shuffle to the right about three steps then shuffle to the left. Repeat this for a time.

Inchworm: Begin by placing your hands on the ground in front of your feet. Walk your hands out into a plank position, and then walk your feet up to your hands. Without standing, walk your hands back out and repeat.

Scissor Skier: Begin by standing, arms at your side. Jump into a high lunge with the opposite arm raised to the leg in the front. Jump again, alternating the arms and legs.

Tricep Dips: Sit on the edge of a chair or other hard surface. Slide your legs out in front of you with your heels resting on the ground.

Push yourself up and off the chair, and lower yourself down in front, as low as you can. Push back up and repeat.

Bridges: Begin by laying on your back and your feet flat on the floor. Engaging your glutes, push your butt off the ground, and form a straight line with your body. A variation is to extend one leg and only push off the ground using one leg.

Clamshells: Lying on one side, stack your legs with your knees bent at a 45 degree angle. Rotate the hip on top to raise the knee off of the bottom. Lower and repeat.

Mountain Climbers: Begin in a plank position. Quickly move your knees towards your elbows, alternating between legs.

Plank Jacks: Begin in a forearm plank position. Step one foot to the side and then bring it back to the center, repeat with the other leg. Continue alternating the legs.

Burpees: From standing, bend over touching the ground, jump back to a plank position, jump your feet back to your hands, and stand. Repeat.

Bicycle Crunches: Lying on your back, raise your legs and shoulders slightly off the ground. Draw opposite knee to opposite elbow and start alternating, like you were peddling a bicycle.

Russian Twist: Sitting on the floor, extend your legs out until you knees are at a 45 degree angle. Lean back slightly, engaging your abs, and rotate your torso from side to side.

Shoulder Taps: Start in a plank position and reach with your right hand to touch your left shoulder, bring your hand back down and repeat with the other.

Touchdowns: From standing, jump into a squat position and reach with one hand to touch the ground. Come back up and repeat with the other hand.

Dead Bug: Begin by lying on your back with hands pointing towards the ceiling and your legs bent at 90 degrees.

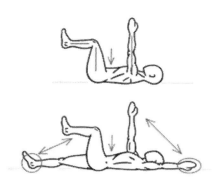

Lower opposite leg and arm towards the floor. The arm should extend behind your head. Bring back up, and repeat with the other side.

Chapter 5: Intermediate Exercises

200 Workout

In this workout, you will be performing a total of 200 reps. There isn't any need for you to do more in the one set unless this felt too easy.

- 40 Leg Raises: 2 sets of 15 (one of each leg), 1 set of 10 (five reps on each leg)
- 40 crunches: 2 sets of 20
- 40 triceps dips: 4 sets of 10
- 40 pushups: 2 sets of 15, 1 set of 10
- 40 jump squats: 2 sets of 20

Sculpt Your Body Workout

Each exercise will tell you how many sets you have to do before moving onto the next. Try not to rest between sets of individual exercises. Rest 30 seconds to a minute between each exercise.

- 60 Second Butt Kicks, 3 Sets
- 45 Second Side Lunge, 3 Sets
- 30 Second Side Plank with Front Kick, 3 Sets each side
- 45 Second Speed Bag Punches, 3 Sets
- 60 Second Side to Side Shuffle, 3 Sets
- 60 Second Squat Kickback, alternating sides, 3 Sets
- 30 Second Side Plank with Hip Abduction, 3 Sets each side
- 45 Second Inchworm, 3 Sets
- 45 Second Scissor Skier, 3 Sets

- 45 Second Crab Kicks, alternating sides, 3 Sets

She Devil

Repeat this circuit of exercise either 3 or 5 times, depending on your skill level. Rest for no more than 2 minutes between each set.

To Failure Tricep Dips

- 40 Punches
- 20 Lunge Punches
- 20 Plank Back Kicks, alternating legs
- 20 Bridges
- 10 Raised Leg Bridges
- 10 Sit-up Punches
- 10 Clamshells, each side
- 10 Sitting Twists

Gladiator

Perform this circuit three or five times, depending on your skill level. Avoid resting between exercises, and rest for no more than two minutes between sets.

- 40 lunges
- 20 jumping lunges
- 20 Squats
- 20 Shoulder taps
- 40 Mountain Climbers
- 10 Pushups
- 10 Up and Down Planks

Full Body Cardio

For these exercises, do two sets of each exercise before moving on. Rest only 30 seconds between each different exercise.

- 15 Superman
- 45 Second Single Leg Glute Bridge
- 45 Second Bicycle Crunches
- 15 Alternating Squat Jumps
- 15 Flutter Kicks
- 15 High Box Jump
- 15 Judo Pushups
- 60 Second Burpees
- 15 Walking Lunges
- 45 Plank Jacks
- 45 Second Mountain Climbers
- 15 Squats

Wake Up Workout

For this circuit, do four to five sets, depending on your skill level. Rest for a minute between each set.

- 10 Burpees
- 15 Pushups
- 20 Mountain Climbers
- 30 Bicycle Crunches
- 45 Second Plank

Refresh

These bodyweight exercises should be repeated three times with a minute rest between sets.

- 15 Lunges
- 15 Squats
- 30 Second Wall Squat

- 60 Second Plank
- 20 Russian Twists
- 20 Jumping Jacks

Extreme Arms

For this workout, pick a number of reps you need to feel challenged, but make sure it's not so hard that you have to take a lot of rests.

You will do a total of five rounds with a minute rest between exercises and two minutes between sets.

Sets One and Three

- 10 Forearm Pushups
- 10 Chin ups
- 15 Diamond Pushups
- Sets Two and Four
- 10 Dips
- 10 to 15 Horizontal Pull Ups, elevated feet, and supinated grip
- Max out Horizontal Pull Up Hold, you should be able to hold it for at least 10 seconds
- Set Five
- Max out Dead Hang

Level Six

For this workout, if you find one set easy, do two sets. If that's still too easy, add more sets or try one of the harder workouts in this book.

- 50 Jumping Jacks
- 15 Squats
- 15 Lunges, each leg

- 60 Russian Twists
- 25 Vertical Leg Crunches
- 10 Burpees
- 10 Oblique Crunches, each side
- 35 Jumping Jacks
- 15 V-Ups
- 15 Tricep Dips
- 20 Standing Calf Raises
- 5 Jump Squats
- 10 Kneeling Pushups
- 30 Second Plank

Power of 10

This one is pretty self-explanatory. There is no need to do more than one set unless this one seems easy.

- 100 Jumping Jacks
- 90 Knee Raises
- 80 Calf Raises
- 70 Side Lunge
- 60 Crunches
- 50 Lunges
- 40 Side to Side Shuffle
- 30 Squats
- 20 Pushups
- 10 Burpees

3 X 100 (Workout)

Do only one set of this workout.

- 100 Mountain Climbers
- 90 Crunches
- 80 Lunges

- 70 Donkey Kicks
- 60 Pushups
- 50 Mountain Climbers
- 40 Crunches
- 30 Lunges
- 20 Donkey Kicks
- 10 Minute Run

Ultimate

Perform four sets of this exercise. Rest for a couple of minutes between sets and 45 seconds between exercises.

- 25 Tricep Dips
- 20 Knee Raises
- 15 Pull Ups
- 25 Squats, alternating legs
- 20 Pushups
- 15 Decline Pushups
- 25 Calf Raises, each leg
- 15 Close Grip Chin Ups

Level Four

This exercise is perfect with just one set, but if you want a little more of a challenge do two sets.

- 35 Jumping Jacks
- 10 Tricep Dips
- 15 Squats
- 5 Knee Push Ups
- 10 Calf Raises
- 35 Russian Twists
- 30 Second Plank
- 10 Second Side Plank, each side

- 30 Jumping Jacks
- 5 Jump Squats
- 5 Knee Pushups
- 5 Burpees

10 to 1 (Workout)

This is a pyramid workout. Begin by doing 10 reps of each exercise, and then start over and 9, 8, 7, and so on until you reach 1.

Mountain Climbers

Touchdowns, alternating hands
Shoulder Taps, alternating hands

- Squat Jumps
- Speed Skaters
- Pushups
- Plank jacks

Muffin Top

For this workout, you will do three sets of each exercise and rest for a minute before moving onto the next exercise.

- 60 Second Run in Place
- 45 Second Bicycle Crunches
- 45 Second Dead Bug
- 60 Second Standing Criss Cross Crunches
- 30 Second Side Plank Hip Lifts, each side
- 45 Second Superman
- 45 Second Inchworm
- 30 Second Side Bends, each side
- 45 Second Russian Twist
- 30 Second Plank

Chapter 6: Advanced

We've covered a lot of bodyweight exercise moves and benefits, but we have one more thing to look at. Many people believe that the only way to build muscles is by lifting weight, so let's break that myth right now.

Bodyweight training is an amazing way to build muscle. There are plenty of people out there who would argue with you about that, and say only free weights can.

A great thing about bodyweight workouts is that they don't hurt your joints like traditional weight training sometimes does. You have a natural motion range and this helps to improve your athleticism overall.

When performing advanced exercises, it requires an unmatched level of tension in the whole body.

This is where you get the amazing strength gain. Even still, you will find people that believe that bodyweight training can't be as effective traditional weight training when you are interested in building muscle.

This is because it is typically associated with the military, endurance, and high reps. But take a look at the upper body of several male gymnasts, and you get a very different picture.

The main reason why people don't have success with bodyweight workouts is because they don't utilize or know the proper way of bodyweight progressions. That leaves them never increasing their resistance.

They are stuck doing the basic versions of inverted rows and pushups and then start thinking it's too easy for it to be building muscles. And they're not wrong.

The basic forms of bodyweight exercises are going to be too easy after a while and won't provide the amount of tension or overload so that you can build muscles.

Now, what if you started working yourself up to one-armed pushups, one-armed inverted rows, or steep incline pushups?

Or you're doing a wide grip inverted row to the neck while your elbows are flared with a two to three-second hold at the top.

Then you get so good that you start piling on weighted vests or chains. At that point, it's not a strict bodyweight workout anymore. At that point, it's bodyweight and resistance.

Even still, it is a variation of bodyweight exercises, and it is very effective.
One of the other reasons why people think weight training is easier to build muscles is because they can progress by grabbing a heavier weight which is easier than progressing from a frog or cow stand to a planche pushup during the next 18 to 24 months.

You have to have a lot of discipline and patience.

Another problem is that while you are gaining muscles and weight with proper nutrition, your bodyweight exercises will become increasingly difficult, preventing you from progressing as quickly. Or you think you aren't progressing as you should, so you give up.

Most trainers out there will tell you that a chin up is better than a pull down when you want to build muscles. Then why are other bodyweight exercises not seen as effective?

Why is a forward lean on a ring dip not seen as effective as a bench press?

Why aren't glute raises just as effective as a leg curl?

I'll argue that they are just as effective. Lack of knowledge about how bodyweight training works and how to progress properly is the main reason why people don't see the results that they want.

You can actually gain muscles quickly if you constantly progress your movements. If you just do several reps, like a lot of people do, that isn't going to help you build muscles.

In order to gain strength and muscle, you have to have a significant amount of load and tension. High reps won't give you either.

You have to activate the fast-twitch fibers in your muscles to build muscles. For the upper body, its best, if your goal is building muscle, to stick with 5 to 12 repetitions with more advanced moves.

When you are working on the lower body, it's okay to go with higher reps to build muscle. 20 reps of pistol squats on each leg are going to create great leg growth.

Once you cover both of those factors, you have to start adding in the right amount of frequency and volume so that you elicit the strength and muscle gains.

Advanced Moves

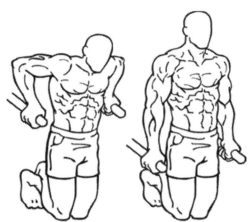

Dips: dips have several variations. For exercises that call for only dips, to perform these you will need a dip bar.

Grip the two bars with your elbows bent above the bars. Push yourself up until your elbows lock and then lower back down. To work your chest, angle yourself forward slightly until you feel a pull in your chest.

For a straight bar dip, you will use a straight bar positioned at about bellybutton height, and push yourself up and down.

Decline Pushups: This is just like a regular pushup, all you have to do is place your feet on an elevated surface.

Diamond Pushups: Another variation of the regular pushup. Place your hands together to form a diamond shape under the center of your chest and perform pushups as you normally would.

Arching Pushups: For this pushup variation, your hips should be lowered closer to the ground, and your feet should be positioned slightly wider than hip width apartment.

Australian Chin Ups: For this variation on the chin up, you will lower yourself under a straight bar with your feet stretched out in front and your heels on the ground.

In and Out Squat Jumps: This is just like a regular squat jump except your alternate from your feet being together and your feet being open.

Pyramid Calf Raises: These are regular one leg calf raises except you have to complete a pyramid of reps. Meaning, if it says 15 then you would start by doing 15 reps on one leg, rest a couple of seconds, and then do 14 reps on the same leg and continue until you reach one, then repeat on the other leg.

Hannibal Squats: These are regular squats but with your feet together.

Pistol Squats: These are one-legged squats. You squat down on one leg and allow the other to stretch out in front of you; make sure it doesn't touch the ground.

Star Jumps: Begin by standing with your feet hip width apart and your arms by your side. Squat slightly and jump up as high as you can; spreading your legs as wide as they can go and reaching your arms up and out. Come back down to neutral and repeat.

Glute Squeezes: These are super simple. Lay face down with your legs slightly wider than hip width apart. Squeeze your glute muscles and raise your legs as high as you can, keeping your upper body on the ground.

Scissor Chops: Standing, raise your arms straight out in front of you, palms facing each other. Begin making a chopping motion with your arms as fast as you can.

Arm Scissors: Standing, raise your arms straight out in front of you, palms facing down. Start swinging your arms across your body; alternating which arm is on top and which is on bottom.

Side V Crunches: This works like a regular V-up except you are on your side.

Begin by lying on your side, the bottom arm extended in front and the other hand behind your head. Using your side muscles, pull your knees and upper elbow towards each other.

Spiderman Planks: Begin in a full plank position and bring your knee out to a 90 degree angle to touch your elbow. Bring that foot back down and repeat with the other leg.

Lying Knee Tucks and Hugs: For tucks, begin by lying flat on you back and engage your abdominal muscles to bring your knees up to your chest. For hugs, begin just like with the tucks, but when you bring you knees in, wrap your arms around them and bring your nose up to touch your knees.

Chapter 7: Advanced Exercises

The following are all advanced exercise routines. There will be a combination of all the previous exercises as well as harder movements.

The important thing here is to make sure that you feel challenged. If the number of reps I have listed is easy for you to do, then up the number of reps, or make a move a little harder. Above all else, listen to your body.

Chest Insanity
Perform four sets of these exercises, resting two minutes between each set. You can stop there, or you can move into another isolation routine for the back or legs.

- 10 straight bar dips
- 10 decline push ups
- 10 arching push ups
- 10 dips
- 5 diamond push ups
- 15 regular push ups

Back Brutality
Perform three sets of these exercises, resting two minutes between each set.

- 5 Upside Down Pull Ups
- 5 Shoulder Width Pull Ups, behind the neck

- 5 Wide Grip Pull Ups, behind the neck
- 5 Close Grip Pull Ups
- 10 Wide Pull Ups

Arm Assassin
Perform five sets of these exercises, resting two minutes between each set.

- 20 Tricep Dips
- 10 Straight Bar Dips
- 20 Close Grip Australian Chin Ups
- 10 Close Grip Chin Ups
- 20 Tricep Dips
- 10 Dips
- 20 Wide Grip Australian Chin Ups
- 10 Shoulder Width Chin Ups

Leg Shocker Routine
Perform five sets of these exercises, resting two minutes between each set.

- 1 minute Wall Sit
- 20 Walking Lunges
- 20 In and Out Squat Jumps
- 15 Pyramid Calf Raises
- 20 Hannibal Squats
- 10 Pistol Squats, per leg

Extreme Full Body
Perform this at least two times. Repeat as many times as you feel you can.

- 1:30 Jog in Place

- 15 V-Ups
- 10 Burpees
- 30 Russian Twists
- 10 Pushups
- 10 Donkey Kicks, per leg
- 45 Second Plank
- 10 Burpees
- 20 Plie Squats
- 15 Reverse Lunges, per leg
- 20 Squats
- 10 Burpees
- 5 Star Jumps
- 40 Jumping Jacks

Timer Workout

This workout doesn't count reps. Instead, you will perform a workout for a specific amount of time.

For a quick seven minute workout, only perform one set. For a 21 minute workout, perform three sets.

Keep track of how many you are able to do in each set, and then compare your numbers the next time you do this workout.

- 40 Seconds of High Knees, alternating legs
- 40 Seconds of Burpees
- 40 Seconds of Plank Jacks
- 40 Seconds of V-Ups
- 40 Seconds of Diamond Pushups
- 40 Seconds of Jump Squats
- 40 Seconds of Lunge with a Front Kick, alternating legs
- 40 Seconds of Leg Lifts

- 40 Seconds of Pistol Squats
- 40 Seconds of Plank Leg Lifts, alternating legs

300 Workout

This one gets its name because you will be doing 300 reps. There's not need to do more than one set unless you are feeling lucky.

- 50 Leg Raises
- 50 Forward Lunges
- 50 Crunches
- 50 Tricep Dips
- 50 Pushups
- 50 Jump Squats

Summer Booty

Only perform one set of these workouts. Do not rest between each exercise unless you absolutely have to.

- 10 Single Leg Glute Bridge, each leg
- 10 Plank Glute Lifts, each leg
- 10 Wall Squats with Leg Circles, each leg
- 50 Alternating Curtsy Lunges
- 50 Alternating Stiff Deadlifts
- 50 Glue Squeezes
- 10 Wall Squats with Leg Circles, each leg
- 10 Plank Glue Lifts, each leg
- 10 Single Leg Glute Bridge, each leg

Running Strength Workout

Repeat this workout circuit three times. This is great for somebody who is training for a marathon or wants to get into running shape.

- ¼ Mile Run
- 15 Squats
- ¼ Mile Run
- 10 Pushups
- ¼ Mile Run
- 10 Dips
- ¼ Mile Run
- 45 Second Plank

Cardio Strength Workout

This is a 15-minute pyramid workout. Only one set is needed. If this is a little too easy for you, start by lowering your squats, choosing a harder pushup variation, and add in 3 burpees after each set of pushups.

- 1 Sumo Squat
- 10 Pushups
- 2 Sumo Squats
- 9 Pushups
- 3 Sumo Squats
- 8 Pushups
- 4 Sumo Squats
- 7 Pushups
- 5 Sumo Squats
- 6 Pushups
- 6 Sumo Squats
- 5 Pushups
- 7 Sumo Squats
- 4 Pushups
- 8 Sumo Squats
- 3 Pushups

- 9 Sumo Squats
- 2 Pushups
- 10 Sumo Squats
- 1 Pushups

Explosive Cardio

Begin by completing three sets of circuit one, rest for a minute, and then complete three sets of circuit two. If 60 seconds and three sets are too easy, increase the time to 90 seconds and four sets.

Circuit One

- 60 Second Forearm Side Plank, repeat on another side
- 60 Second Mountain Climbers
- 60 Second Burpees

Circuit Two

- 60 Second Jump Squats
- 60 Second Squats
- 60 Second Jumping Lunges, alternating sides
- 60 Second Lunges, alternating sides

Cardio HIIT

For this workout, you will be doing an exercise as quickly as you can for 20 seconds then resting for 10 before moving onto the next exercise.

Depending on your skill level you can do 5, 7, or 10 sets. Rest for two minutes between each set.

- 20 Second High Knees
- 20 Second Punches

- 20 Second Plank with Jab Cross
- 20 Second High Knees
- 20 Second Punches
- 20 Second Plank Jack with Jab Cross

*Do a pushup between each exercise

Power HIIT

For this one, like the last, you can choose between 5, 7, or 10 sets depending on your skill level. Rest for two minutes between each set.

- 20 Second Squats
- 20 Second Plank Walk-Outs
- 20 Second Scissor Chops
- 20 Second Squats
- 20 Second Pushups
- 20 Second Arm Scissors

*Do a squat jump between each exercise.

Crazy Legs

There are four circuits in this workout. You will do four rounds of each circuit with minimal rest between each set. Rest for a minute between each circuit.

Circuit One

- 20 Second Mountain Climbers
- 10 Second Rest
- 20 Second Pushups
- 10 Second Rest

Circuit Two

- 20 Second Side Lunge

- 10 Second Rest
- 20 Second Squats
- 10 Second rest

Circuit Three

- 20 Second High Knees
- 10 Second Rest
- 20 Second Jumping Jacks
- 10 Second Rest

Circuit Four

- 20 Second Burpees
- 10 Second Rest
- 20 Second Flutter Kicks
- 10 Second Rest

High Energy

For this one, rest for 30 seconds between each circuit. You only have to do one set, but if this feels to easy, start adding more sets until it becomes a challenge.

Circuit One

- 10 Crunches
- 10 Squats
- 10 Jumping Jacks

Circuit Two

- 30 Second Plank
- 7 Pushups
- 25 High Knees, one rep equals two knee raises

Circuit Three

- 12 Crunches
- 10 Lunges, each leg
- 7 Burpees

Circuit Four

- 30 Second Plank
- 12 Dips
- 25 Jumping Jacks

Circuit Five

- 12 Crunches
- 15 Squats
- 25 High Knees

Circuit Six

- 30 Second Plank
- 5 Pushups
- 10 Burpees

Core Blast

Do the following exercise with no rest. Do two sets with a minute rest between sets.

- 50 Scissor Kicks
- 15 Knee Hugs
- 50 Windshield Wipers
- 15 Lying Knee Tucks
- 50 Elbow Plank Butt Ups
- 15 Left Side V Crunches

- 50 Spiderman Planks, alternating legs
- 15 Right Side V Crunches

Conclusion

Thank you for making it through to the end of *Bodyweight Training*. Let's hope it was informative and able to provide you with all of the tools you need to achieve your goals of starting a bodyweight training routine.

The next step is to start using what you have learned. Decide whether you're a beginner, intermediate, or advanced and pick a few of the routines given in this book. All it takes is at least three workouts each week.

Finally, if you found this book useful in any way, a review on Amazon is always appreciated!

Made in the USA
Middletown, DE
26 November 2018